Spoon Desserts!

Custards, Crèmes, *&* Elegant Fruit Desserts

by Lynn Nusom

Specialty Cookbook Series Edited by Andrea Chesman

The Crossing Press • Freedom • California 95019

This book is dedicated to my wife, Guylyn Morris Nusom, a great cook, who has seen this project through from beginning to end.

Special thanks to Virginia White, Ellen Lively Steele, and Andrea Chesman, my editor, who helped shape the book as it is today.

Cover illustration and design by Alpha Bets Design
Interior illustrations by Melanie Lofland Gendron

Printed in the U.S.A.

Library of Congress Cataloging-in-Publication Data

Nusom, Lynn.
    Spoon desserts! : custards, cremes, & elegant fruit desserts / by
Lynn Nusom.
        p.   cm. — (Specialty cookbook series)
    Includes indes.
    ISBN 0-89594-446-4 (cloth)   ISBN 0-89594-445-6 (pbk)
    1. Desserts.   I. Title.   II. Series.
TX773.N87 1990
641.8'6—dc20
                        90-40534
                        CIP

Contents

Introduction 1

1. Elegant Fruit Desserts 7

2. Sabayons, Custards, & Crèmes 19

3. Fruit with Sabayons, Custards, & Crèmes 37

4. Mousses 57

5. Baked Custards, Flans, & Puddings 77

6. Bread & Rice Puddings 95

7. Steamed Puddings 105

8. Dessert Sauces 113

Index 131

Introduction

❖❖

Desserts conjure up different mental images for different people. Lately most people turn down dessert offerings in restaurants, afraid that the folks they are dining with will think they don't care about their health and/or their waistlines.

Cooks skip over the dessert pages in their favorite cookbook, hoping they are doing their family a favor by depriving them of that traditional last course. Or if they do serve something, it is often something joyless and unappealing, because they think that deprivation is good for the soul.

Yet most of us still crave that wonderful taste of something sweet after a meal. True; pies, cakes, tarts, and pastries, such as Napoleons, have their time and place. These are what I call "fork food." Fork food is often formal food. If you serve something after dinner that requires a spoon, the conversation around the table gets more relaxed, and everyone feels better.

There can be something very elegant about gently dipping a spoon into a lovely looking cream, or custard surrounded by a colorful sauce. What could be more attractive than a Chocolate Bavarian Cream on top of a Raspberry Sauce?

I have given recipes in this book for so-called comfort desserts as well as the more elegant ones, all to be eaten with a spoon. However, even the most elegant of these desserts is easy to prepare. I firmly believe cooking should be a happy experience, so I strive to create recipes that are as simple to make as possible.

Spicy ethnic foods are extremely popular and a great help in putting a little zip into our menu planning. Nothing tops off a meal of chili or curry dishes better than the clean, bright taste of one of the fruit desserts in chapter 1.

Finding the best fruit is often daunting to many shoppers. Selecting berries of any kind, especially when one is a long distance from the growing area, can be tricky. A couple of tips. Remember when buying strawberries that they don't ripen after they are picked. Be sure to buy the plumpest, shiniest, nicest red ones you can find. Make sure that they are free of mold and the brown scars that show up from time to time. I know it's hard to check, as they are so often packaged in those little containers, covered with plastic wrap and secured with rubber bands. Very often the top berries look perfect, but they may be hiding some inferior cousins underneath.

When you get the berries home, if you are not going to use them right away, store them in the refrigerator. Don't wash them before you put them in the refrigerator as that will shorten their shelf life.

The largest, prettiest berries of all kinds are not always the sweetest. Try sampling one before you buy.

If you gently shake the container and the berries move freely, they are usually fresh. The older ones tend to become packed tight and are often moldy, which prevents them from moving around in the box.

Raspberries are extremely fragile. I find it wise to check with the produce people to see if the berries just arrived in their store, and/or if they have had any complaints. Very often the produce clerk will get you a box from the freshest shipment. If you shop at one particular store all the time, you may find that a present of a few homemade cookies or candy to the folks in the produce department from time to time goes a long way in helping get the best fruit for your money.

In addition to the recipes in this book, try different combinations of fruit with perhaps a splash of your favorite liqueur, brandy, bourbon, or sweet wine. Or you can add any of these to whipped cream (1 to 2 tablespoons to 1 cup of whipped cream). It will give the cream a totally different taste.

Heavy cream whips best when it is a few days old. Have the cream as cold as possible. Put the bowl and the beaters in the refrigerator to chill before you begin. Cream will form peaks faster if you beat it in a small bowl with steep sides.

At our house, we like to serve fresh fruit in glass bowls, or on glass plates. The natural colors are a delight to the eye, especially when laced with a little sabayon or a complementing sauce. Wine glasses are also wonderful containers for the spoon desserts in these pages. The longer the stem the better. Collecting interesting one-of-a-kind wine or champagne glasses is fun. It's an interesting way to serve dessert at an informal buffet or party.

Creams, or crèmes in French, are the basis for many elegant desserts. A small serving of a cream, especially napped with a heavenly sauce, can soothe the savage beast in anyone, erasing the tensions of the day.

Custard is a broad family of desserts that includes flans, zabaglione, and sabayons, as well as the more traditional American cup custard. Zabaglione is the Italian name for a rich, sweet custard usually served warm. Zabaglione can be made with all sorts of sweet wines or liqueurs.

The most popular seem to be Madeira, rum, port, sherry, or brandy. Sabayon is the French word for a very similar, slightly lighter dessert usually made with wine. Sabayons can be served either warm or chilled and are excellent with fresh fruit.

A lot of desserts are labeled mousses. Many of these are just packaged puddings masquerading under what some people think is a fancier sounding name. A true mousse is a delightful dish that can be anything from an appetizer to a main luncheon course, to a simply wonderful dessert.

Mousse is the French word for moss. It is used to describe a dish that is soft and very, very light. With few exceptions mousses are made with beaten egg whites and whipped cream. They can be as varied in flavor as the imagination of the cook creating them. Chapter 4 has just a few examples.

To me the bread, and rice puddings in chapter 6, and the steamed puddings in chapter 7 are the ultimate comfort foods.

Puddings come to us from a simpler time and were probably one of man's first culinary accomplishments, no doubt evolving from porridges and gruels. The word *pudding* was used as early as the fourteenth century to describe a dish that resembled a sausage. Various internal parts of an animal were stuffed with a mixture of ground grains and/or meat.

Then puddings came to embrace a wide array of soft foods, very often wrapped in a flour paste and steamed or boiled in a pudding bag. These bags were made of muslin or knitted from cotton yarn. The latter looked like a man's stocking cap. Pudding bags were used in America in the eighteenth and nineteenth centuries, and are still used in Ireland and England today. The housewives in colonial America rubbed the outside of the bag with lard, dipped it into boiling water, floured it, and then turned the bag to the inside out and filled it with the pudding batter. The bags were only half full to allow the pudding to swell.

The puddings were then either put into boiling water or steamed on top of vegetables cooking in huge black iron kettles. Many cooks made a new bag every time they made a pudding. More frugal ones used the same bag over and over. It was a real job cleaning pudding bags, but the cooks of the day reasoned the resulting treats were worth it.

At one time in the history of puddings, they were served as the first course of a dinner. There is an old saying that went, "I came early in pudding time." Another, less kind saying was about little boys who were too fat and were called "pudding bags." In the Dickensian era, all respectable Englishmen finished off their meals with a pudding.

With the arrival of the easy instant puddings in a box, pudding making in this country almost became a lost art, but it's staging a comeback now.

The finishing touch to many of the desserts in these pages is the right sauce. I have suggested sauces for several of the dishes, but please try interchanging them or using two sauces with one dessert. This can be especially colorful when you spread one sauce on half of a dessert plate, and the other sauce on the remaining half, with the custard, cream, or pudding placed in the center.

I am particularly fond of the visual effects of spreading the sauces on a dessert plate and then either unmolding or spooning the dessert on top of the sauce, usually to one side, so that the color of the sauce shows through.

For a brilliant, colorful effect, put a little whipped cream, another sauce, or some all-fruit preserves of a contrasting color in a line or two on top of the original sauce. Take a knife and make a design in the sauce before putting the cream or pudding onto the plate.

Try these spoon desserts for a touch of elegance and a spoonful of comfort in your life.

1
Elegant Fruit Desserts

Strawberries and Kiwi with Lemon Curd

Lemon curd is just a little bit of heaven on earth. It can be served with other sliced fresh fruits, berries, or preserves. Lemon curd also makes a great base for Napoleons and other pastries and can be used as a filling for cakes.

1 cup butter, at room temperature
Juice of 3 lemons
Grated zest of 1 lemon
2 cups sugar
6 eggs, beaten
1 pint strawberries
2 kiwis
Garnish: Shaved semisweet chocolate

Combine the butter, lemon juice, lemon zest, and sugar in the top of a double boiler. Stir the ingredients until blended. Stir in the eggs. Place over boiling water and cook for about 20 minutes, beating continually with a wire whisk until the mixture becomes very thick. Cool; then chill in the refrigerator for at least 2 hours.

Spoon the lemon curd into 4 individual glass dessert dishes, reserving 4 teaspoons as topping.

Wash, hull, and slice the strawberries. Peel and thinly slice the kiwis. Arrange the fruit on top of the lemon curd. Top each dish with a teaspoon of the remaining curd, garnish with shaved chocolate, and serve.

Yield: 4 servings

Strawberries Romanoff

❖❖❖

The original version of this is attributed to Antonin Carême, who was the chef at the court of Czar Alexander I of Russia. The Czar, tired of the standard desserts being served to his guests, asked Carême to come up with something different on short notice. The famous French chef had some strawberries and cream on hand. He added some brandy and liqueur for a dessert that has inspired cooks ever since. This is my version.

1 pint large ripe strawberries, washed and hulled
2 tablespoons sugar
2 tablespoons Grand Marnier
1 tablespoon cognac

1 cup whipping cream
2 teaspoons sugar
1 teaspoon Grand Marnier

Lightly toss the strawberries with the 2 tablespoons sugar, 2 tablespoons Grand Marnier, and cognac in a small bowl. Refrigerate for at least 1 hour and then spoon into 4 stemmed dessert dishes or champagne glasses.

Just before serving, whip the cream until it starts to stiffen. Add the remaining 2 teaspoons sugar and 1 teaspoon Grand Marnier and continue beating the cream until stiff. Spoon over the strawberries and serve.

Yield: 4 servings

Benedictine Strawberries

*Benedictine is created from very good cognac brandy to which a selection of herbs is added. The D.O.M. on each label is the motto of the Benedictine Order—*Deo Optimo Maximo—*To God, Most Good, Most Great.*

2 cups milk
⅛ teaspoon salt
¼ cup sugar
¼ cup Benedictine liqueur
6 egg yolks
¼ cup whipping cream
2 pints ripe strawberries, washed and
  hulled
Garnish: Powdered sugar

Combine the milk, salt, and sugar in the top of a double boiler. Heat over hot water until the milk is too hot to touch. Then stir in the Benedictine.

Beat together the egg yolks and the whipping cream. Gradually add to the milk mixture. Cook, stirring constantly, until sauce thickens. Take the pan off the hot water. Continue to stir as the mixture cools.

Arrange the strawberries in a 2-quart porcelain soufflé dish, reserving a few for the garnish. Pour the egg/milk mixture over the strawberries and chill.

To serve, unmold onto a serving platter and garnish with the remaining fresh strawberries dusted with powdered sugar.

Yield: 4 servings

Lime Curd with Cantaloupe and Raspberries

❖❖❖

We have made lemon curd for years, but never lime curd. The motivation was simple—we were out of lemons, and limes were on sale that week. I had never come across a recipe for lime curd so we made it up as we went along. It has a much more delicate flavor than lemon curd and is the perfect backdrop for fruit.

6 limes
⅓ cup butter
1 cup sugar
2 eggs, beaten
1 teaspoon grated orange zest
½ pint raspberries
1 medium-sized cantaloupe, peeled, seeded, and thinly sliced

Juice the limes, and combine the juice with the butter and sugar in the top of a double boiler. Cook over hot water until the sugar dissolves. Stir in the eggs, along with the orange zest. Cook, stirring constantly, until nicely thickened. Cool; then chill in the refrigerator for at least 2 hours.

Arrange the cantaloupe slices in a fan shape on one side of 6 to 8 large dessert plates. Spoon the lime curd onto the other side. Mound the raspberries between the cantaloupe slices and the lime curd, saving a few of the nicest berries to put on top of the lime curd. Serve at once.

Yield: 6 to 8 servings

Blackberries à la the Viscount

◆◆◆

A friend of mine loved his sweets and his booze, especially after the doctor told him that they were both forbidden! When he visited us in New York, he always asked me to make rich desserts, especially ones with liquor in them.

1½ tablespoons unflavored gelatin
2 tablespoons cold water
6 tablespoons boiling water
1 cup sugar
⅓ cup dark rum
¼ cup Irish whiskey
3 egg whites
1 cup whipping cream
1 pint blackberries
Garnish: Whipped cream and sliced
   almonds

Soften the gelatin in the cold water; then add the boiling water and stir until the gelatin is dissolved. Add the sugar, rum, and Irish whiskey, and beat until frothy.

Beat the egg whites until they form stiff peaks. Fold them into the gelatin mixture. Beat the whipping cream until stiff and fold in.

Pick over and wash the blackberries. Divide equally among 4 individual serving dishes. Pour the cream mixture over them and chill for at least 1 hour in the refrigerator. Serve with a dollop of whipped cream and a sprinkling of sliced almonds.

Yield: 4 servings

Jamaican Bananas

❖❖❖

The secret of cooking bananas is to use very firm, almost green bananas and cook over high heat for a short time. The longer they stay on the heat, the mushier they tend to get.

1 cup whipping cream
¼ cup powdered sugar
¼ cup dark rum
1 teaspoon vanilla extract
4 large firm bananas
¼ cup butter
¼ teaspoon ground cloves
¼ teaspoon ground cinnamon
¼ teaspoon ground nutmeg
¼ cup firmly packed light brown sugar
2 tablespoons dried, sweetened
  coconut, lightly toasted

Beat the cream until it starts to form peaks. Add the powdered sugar and beat until thick. Fold in the rum and the vanilla.

Peel and cut the bananas into quarters lengthwise.

Melt the butter in a sauté pan or frying pan; stir in the cloves, cinnamon, nutmeg, and brown sugar. Add the bananas and sauté over high heat until the bananas are golden brown.

Arrange in 4 serving dishes, top with the whipped cream, sprinkle with coconut, and serve.

Note: To toast the coconut, preheat the oven to 325° F. Spread the coconut in a thin layer on a baking sheet. Toast for 5 to 8 minutes, shaking the pan every few minutes.

Yield: 4 servings

Jungle Cry

❖❖

I served this at a dinner party one evening and a male guest with a touch too much of the bubbly under his belt let out a Tarzan yell of delight at the taste, hence the name!

6 firm, ripe bananas
1 tablespoon melted butter
¼ cup dark rum
¼ cup firmly packed light brown sugar
1 cup whipping cream
2 tablespoons white sugar
1 cup shredded, dried, sweetened
　coconut
½ teaspoon raspberry liqueur

Preheat the oven to 375° F. Lightly butter a shallow baking dish.

Peel the bananas; slice lengthwise and then in half horizontally. Place in the baking dish. Brush the bananas with the melted butter, pour the rum over top, then sprinkle with the brown sugar. Bake for 10 minutes, or until the bananas are tender.

While the bananas bake, whip the cream, adding the white sugar halfway through. Fold in the coconut and the raspberry liqueur. Arrange the bananas in 6 to 8 individual dessert dishes, top with the whipped cream, and serve.

Yield: 6 to 8 servings

Bananas with Butterscotch

1 cup light brown sugar
1 tablespoon heavy cream
4 tablespoons butter
4 firm, ripe bananas
Garnish: Whipped cream laced with
  bourbon

Combine the brown sugar, heavy cream, and butter in a saucepan and cook over low heat until the sugar melts and the mixture begins to bubble. Peel and slice each banana into an individual serving dish, pour the butterscotch over the banana slices, and serve warm, topped with bourbon-flavored whipped cream.

Yield: 4 servings

15

Triple Orange Threat

❖❖❖

The layering of the orange-flavored liqueur with the oranges, orange juice, and orange peel produces a spectacular orange dessert.

2 tablespoons orange zest
¾ cup freshly squeezed orange juice
6 egg yolks, beaten
¼ cup sugar
2 tablespoons Triple Sec
3 seedless oranges, peeled and sectioned
Garnish: 2 teaspoons grated orange zest
   and twisted orange peel

Combine the 2 tablespoons orange zest, orange juice, egg yolks, and sugar in the top of a double boiler, and cook over hot water for 10 minutes, beating with a whisk, until the mixture has tripled in volume. Remove from the heat and plunge the top of the double boiler into a bowl of ice cubes. Beat the mixture until it cools to room temperature. Stir in the Triple Sec.

Arrange the orange sections in 6 individual dessert dishes and top with the Triple Sec mixture. Garnish each serving with some of the 2 teaspoons orange zest and twisted orange peels and serve.

Yield: 6 servings

Minted Grapes

❖❖

I once worked in the motion picture industry and had a brief encounter with Mae West. She was known for her great movie quips, and my favorite has always been when she said, "Beulah, . . . peel me a grape!" in I'm No Angel. *The subject of food did not come up in the course of our conversation, but I can never eat grapes without thinking about Miss West. You don't have to peel the grapes for this recipe—it'll be a smash hit anyway.*

1 cup sour cream
½ cup firmly packed light brown sugar
2 tablespoons white crème de menthe
3 cups green seedless grapes, cut into
   halves
Garnish: Lime slices

Mix together the sour cream, brown sugar, and crème de menthe. Fold in the grape halves and chill in the refrigerator overnight. Serve garnished with slices of fresh lime.

Yield: 4 servings

Pears René

❖❖

I'm always looking for elegant dishes that are easy to make, or that can be done ahead, and yet look and taste as though you spent hours preparing them. This is one such recipe. Even the Chocolate Caramel Sauce can be made ahead and warmed in the microwave just before you are ready to serve the dessert.

½ cup sugar
2 cups water
4 large firm pears
Chocolate Caramel Sauce (page 122),
   heated
¼ cup chopped pecans

Mix together the sugar and water in a large frying or sauté pan over low heat. Peel, halve, and core the pears. Place the pears in the pan and poach until barely tender. Cool; then place face down on a refrigerator tray and freeze.

When you're ready to serve, place the frozen pear halves on 4 small dessert plates, pour the hot Chocolate Caramel Sauce over them, and sprinkle with chopped pecans.

Yield: 4 servings

2
Sabayons, Custards, & Crèmes

Sabayon

❖❖❖

Sabayon is a wine-egg sauce that can be served with puddings or fruit, or it can be served as a dessert in its own right. Sabayon is especially good when accompanied by a rich cookie. Easy-to-make sabayons are flavored with various wines and liqueurs. The French use white wine, champagne, or Burgundy. Nontraditional cooks will substitute rum, kirsch, or brandy.

6 egg yolks
¾ cup sugar
¾ cup cream sherry

In the top of a double boiler, beat the egg yolks and sugar with a wire whisk until smooth. Place over hot water and add the sherry. Cook and continue beating vigorously until the mixture is light and frothy and has almost doubled in volume.

Place the top of the double boiler in a bowl of ice water and whisk the mixture until cool. Pour into 4 individual serving dishes or stemmed wine glasses and serve at once.

Yield: 4 servings

Zabaglione

❖❖

6 egg yolks
6 teaspoons sugar
¾ cup Marsala wine

In the top of a double boiler, beat the egg yolks and sugar with a wire whisk until smooth. Place over hot water and add the Marsala. Beat again. Cook, beating constantly, for 5 minutes, or until the mixture starts to thicken and almost doubles in volume. Do not let it boil.

Remove from the heat and place the top of the double boiler in a bowl of ice water and whisk the mixture until cool. Pour into 6 glass dessert dishes or stemmed wine glasses and serve at once.

Yield: 6 servings

Pots de Crème

❖❖

Some say that this is the crème de la crème of French desserts. No pun intended! The trick here is the coffee you use. By using a flavored coffee, such as Seville orange, chocolate, or Amaretto, you can subtly change the taste of the dish.

4 ounces semisweet chocolate morsels
3½ teaspoons strong brewed coffee
2½ teaspoons sugar
2 eggs
2 teaspoons brandy
1 cup heavy cream
Garnish: Orange zest

Combine the chocolate morsels, coffee, sugar, eggs, and brandy in a blender and blend until the chocolate morsels are finely ground. Heat the cream just to the boiling point, but do not let it boil. Cool for a few minutes; then pour the cream into the blender and blend again until the mixture is smooth. Spoon the mixture into 6 individual dessert dishes or cups, sprinkle with a little orange zest, and chill before serving.

Yield: 6 servings

Bourbon Custard

❖❖❖

4 egg yolks
¼ cup sugar
⅛ teaspoon salt
¼ teaspoon ground nutmeg
⅛ teaspoon ground mace
1¾ cups milk
¼ cup good bourbon
½ cup raspberry jam
1 cup heavy cream
1 tablespoon sugar

Beat the egg yolks in a saucepan. Then add the ¼ sugar, salt, nutmeg, and mace; beat again. Add the milk and cook over low heat, stirring constantly, until the mixture starts to thicken. Remove from the heat and stir in the bourbon. Pour into 6 to 8 individual dessert dishes. Chill in the refrigerator for 3 to 4 hours.

When the custard is chilled, spread the jam on top of the custard. Beat the cream, adding the remaining 1 tablespoon sugar about halfway through, until it forms stiff peaks. Then spoon it over the top of the custard and serve.

Yield: 6 to 8 servings

Crème Brûlée

❖❖

My mother was in charge of making the maple sugar from the maple syrup my father made every year. I remember that she started making the sugar in a very old wringer washing machine. The agitator had just the right motion to whip the syrup, and the tub was big enough to make a commercial batch. This is one of the ways we used the sugar that wasn't considered fine enough to send to the stores. If you can't find maple sugar, substitute brown sugar.

3 tablespoons light brown sugar
2 cups heavy cream
4 egg yolks, beaten
3 tablespoons crushed maple sugar or
   brown sugar

Mix together the 3 tablespoons light brown sugar and cream in the top of a double boiler set over hot water. Bring just to a boil. Add the egg yolks, a little at a time, stirring constantly. Continue to cook until the mixture is thick enough to coat a spoon. Do not overcook or it will curdle. Cool. Pour into 6 individual custard cups and chill in the refrigerator until set.

Sprinkle the crushed maple sugar on top of each cup of custard, and place under the broiler until the sugar melts. Don't let the sugar burn! Cool; then return to the refrigerator to chill thoroughly before serving.

Yield: 6 servings

Frozen Rum Cream

❖❖

4 egg yolks
¼ cup sugar
3 egg whites
½ teaspoon cream of tartar
1½ cups whipping cream
½ cup dark rum
Garnish: Fresh mint sprigs

Beat the egg yolks in the top of a double boiler over hot water. Add the sugar and continue cooking, beating constantly, until the mixture has thickened. Remove from the heat and cool.

Beat the egg whites until they start to form peaks. Add the cream of tartar and continue beating until the whites are stiff.

Beat the whipping cream until it forms stiff peaks. Fold the egg whites and the whipping cream into the custard. Gently stir in the rum. Pour into 8 individual Pyrex® cups and freeze. Serve garnished with sprigs of fresh mint.

Yield: 8 servings

Madeira Cream

❖❖

Madeira is a somewhat sweet fortified wine similar to port except that it is made from sugarcane. It has a slightly burnt taste that makes it a perfect coupling with certain nuts and fruit. Made for over 4 centuries on the island of Madeira off the coast of Africa, this wine has an aroma that seems to suggest an exotic world. Perhaps that is why it was very popular with the genteel nineteenth century ladies of England and New Orleans, who were fond of sipping the wine along with a piece of cake in the afternoon.

⅓ **cup Madeira wine**
½ **cup golden raisins**
½ **cup chopped pitted dates**

2 **cups milk**
6 **tablespoons all-purpose flour**
⅓ **cup sugar**
½ **teaspoon salt**
1 **whole egg**
2 **egg yolks**
½ **cup chopped pecans**
¼ **teaspoon ground cinnamon**
½ **teaspoon vanilla extract**
1 **cup heavy cream**

Heat the wine over very low heat until it's barely warm. Remove from the heat. Stir in the raisins and dates and set aside.

In a saucepan over medium heat, combine the milk with the flour, sugar, and salt and beat with a wire whisk until smooth.

❖❖

Continue to cook until the mixture comes to a boil. Boil for 2 minutes and then remove from the heat. Beat the egg with the egg yolks. Add a tablespoon of the milk mixture to the eggs and beat again. Mix the rest of the milk mixture into the eggs and return to the heat. Cook until thick, stirring constantly. Remove from the heat; stir in the wine, raisin, and date mixture. Stir in the pecans, cinnamon, and vanilla and set aside to cool.

Whip the cream until stiff and fold into the cooled pudding. Spoon into 8 individual serving dishes and chill for a least 4 hours before serving.

Yield: 8 servings

Rich Chocolate Custard

I can't imagine anything much better in the world of food than good chocolate pudding. Eaten at bedtime it beats sleeping pills hands down.

3 ounces bittersweet chocolate
1 cup sugar
1 tablespoon all-purpose flour
¼ teaspoon salt
2 cups milk
6 egg yolks, beaten
½ teaspoon vanilla extract
Garnish: Shaved white chocolate

Melt the bittersweet chocolate in the top of a double boiler over hot water. Mix together the sugar, flour, and salt and add to the melted chocolate.

Scald 1 cup of the milk, then stir into the chocolate. Beat until smooth. Cook over low heat until the mixture comes to a boil, stirring constantly.

Scald the remaining 1 cup milk and very slowly stir into the beaten egg yolks. Stir into the chocolate mixture. Cook for 3 minutes over boiling water. Remove from the heat and stir in the vanilla. Spoon into 6 individual dessert dishes and chill. Garnish with shaved white chocolate.

Yield: 6 servings

Caribbean Chocolate Custard

❖❖

8 ounces semisweet chocolate, finely
   grated
1 cup heavy cream
1 cup milk
6 egg yolks, lightly beaten
2 tablespoons dark rum
Garnish: Whipped cream and chocolate
   curls

Mix the chocolate with the cream and the milk in the top of a double boiler and cook over hot water, stirring occasionally, for 15 minutes (do not allow it to boil). Cool to room temperature.

Slowly add the eggs into the cooled chocolate mixture, beating constantly. Stir in the rum. Pour into 4 to 6 dessert dishes and chill. Serve with dollops of whipped cream topped with shaved chocolate curls.

Yield: 4 to 6 servings

Chocolate Bavarian Cream

4 egg yolks
¾ cup sugar
1 envelope unflavored gelatin
2 tablespoons cold water
1⅓ cups milk
3 ounces semisweet chocolate
3 tablespoons cognac
1 teaspoon vanilla extract
1½ cups heavy cream
Apricot Sauce (page 116)

Beat the egg yolks with the sugar until smooth. Set aside.

In a small bowl, soften the gelatin in the water. In a saucepan, bring the milk just to a boil and mix 2 tablespoons of the hot milk with the gelatin. Then mix the gelatin into the hot milk and stir well. When the gelatin is dissolved, add the milk mixture to the egg and sugar mixture. Pour into the saucepan and cook over low heat, stirring constantly, until the custard is thick enough to coat the back of a spoon. Cool.

Melt the chocolate in a microwave oven or over very low heat. Add the cognac and vanilla and mix well. Stir into the cooled custard.

Whip the cream until it forms stiff peaks;

❖❖

then fold into the custard. Spoon into 6 to 8 individual molds and chill in the refrigerator until set.

To serve, cover 6 to 8 dessert plates with Apricot Sauce. Unmold the creams and place to one side of the plate, so that the color of the sauce shows well.

Yield: 6 to 8 servings

Kahlua Cream

‡‡

Living near the Mexican border, we have easy, inexpensive access to Kahlua and use it a lot. Here is a light dessert that uses this liqueur. If you can't get Kahlua, use crème de cacao.

1 package orange-flavored gelatin
1 cup heavy cream
1 tablespoon sugar
¼ cup Kahlua
Garnish: Lime twists

Make the gelatin according to the package directions. Refrigerate just until it starts to set up.

Whip the cream until it starts to stiffen, then add the sugar and Kahlua and continue beating until stiff. Fold into the gelatin mixture. Spoon into 4 individual dessert dishes or stemmed goblets and chill in the refrigerator. Garnish each dish with a twist of lime and serve.

Yield: 4 servings

Almond Custard

❖❖❖

For those folks who think custard is too smooth, the almonds in this recipe give the pudding a nice crunch. The best way I've found to grind the almonds is in a coffee grinder or a blender.

2 cups heavy cream
½ teaspoon ground cinnamon
⅓ cup ground blanched almonds
½ cup sugar
1 egg
5 egg yolks
2 tablespoons brandy
Garnish: Thinly sliced almonds

Combine the cream and cinnamon in a saucepan and bring just to a boil. Stir in the almonds and sugar. Remove from the heat.

Beat the whole egg with the egg yolks in a separate saucepan and cook over low heat for 5 minutes. Stir into the hot cream mixture. Cook, stirring constantly, until the custard coats a spoon. Stir in the brandy and pour into 6 individual dessert dishes or custard cups. Garnish with thinly sliced almonds and chill in the refrigerator before serving.

Yield: 6 servings

Floating Island #1

❖❖❖

6 egg yolks
½ cup sugar
3 cups milk
1 tablespoon dark rum
6 egg whites
2 tablespoons sugar
1 cup milk
1 cup sugar

Beat the egg yolks with the ½ cup sugar in the top of a double boiler. Scald the 3 cups milk in a saucepan and add to the egg yolks a little at a time, stirring constantly. Cook over hot water until the custard coats a spoon. Cool; then stir in the rum. Pour into 8 individual dessert dishes, cover, and chill in the refrigerator.

Beat the egg whites until frothy, and then beat in the 2 tablespoons sugar. Heat the remaining 1 cup milk until it starts to bubble. Drop large tablespoons of the egg white mixture into the milk. Poach for 2 minutes, remove with a slotted spoon, and chill in the refrigerator for 2 hours.

Melt the remaining 1 cup sugar in a cast iron skillet over high heat. When it begins

◆◆◆

to melt, tilt the skillet back and forth and keep the sugar moving. When the sugar is fully melted and a light brown color, quickly pour it into a small pitcher.

Place one of the egg white "islands" on the top of each custard, drizzle the caramelized sugar over each, and serve.

Yield: 8 servings

Floating Island #2

❖❖

This is an easier version of floating island.

½ cup sugar
½ teaspoon salt
1 tablespoon cornstarch
2 cups milk
5 egg yolks, beaten
1 teaspoon vanilla extract
5 egg whites
⅓ cup sugar

Mix the ½ cup sugar with the salt and cornstarch in a saucepan. Scald the milk and pour over the sugar mixture very slowly, stirring constantly. Stir in the egg yolks and cook slowly until the custard thickens and coats a spoon. Cool; stir in vanilla.

Beat the egg whites until they start to form peaks, then gradually beat in the remaining ⅓ cup sugar until they form stiff peaks. Fold the egg whites into the custard very, very carefully. Do not break up the egg whites into small pieces.

Spoon into 6 custard cups or dessert dishes and chill for at least 2 hours. The whites will float through the custard and look like small islands, hence the name.

Yield: 6 servings

3
Fruit with Sabayons, Custards, & Crèmes

◆◆

Melon with Rum Sabayon

1 medium-sized Casaba melon
1 medium-sized honeydew melon
6 egg yolks
½ cup sugar
Juice and grated zest of 1 lemon
1 cup dark rum
Garnish: Mint sprigs

Peel and seed the melons and use a melon baller or teaspoon to carve balls out of the flesh. Place the melon balls in 6 individual dessert dishes.

In the top of a double boiler, beat the egg yolks and the sugar until pale and frothy. Add the lemon juice, lemon zest, and rum. Beat well, then cook over hot water for about 10 minutes, stirring constantly with a whisk, until the mixture is thick and creamy. Cool slightly. Pour over the melon balls, garnish with sprigs of mint, and serve.

Yield: 6 servings

Black Cherries with Zabaglione

6 eggs
¼ cup powdered sugar
⅛ teaspoon salt
⅓ cup Marsala wine
1 pound ripe black cherries, pitted
   and halved

In the top of a double boiler, combine the eggs, sugar, and salt. Add the Marsala and cook over hot water, beating constantly, for approximately 10 minutes, or until the mixture is thick. Chill in the refrigerator for at least 3 hours.

Arrange the cherry halves in the bottom of 4 individual stemmed glass dessert dishes, reserving some for the garnish. Spoon the zabaglione over the cherries, garnish with the remaining cherry halves, and serve.

Yield: 4 servings

Fresh Figs with Rum Cream

❖❖❖

Mentioned many times in the Bible, figs are wonderfully rich in taste and are extremely nutritious. When buying figs in the supermarket make sure they are soft and plump. The skin can be purple, brown, or green depending on the variety. The riper the fig, the softer to the touch. Do not buy fresh figs that have a sour smell. This means that the sugar in the fig has fermented and, therefore, the fig is spoiled.

1 envelope unflavored gelatin
1¾ cups milk
⅓ cup sugar
Dash salt
3 eggs, separated
2 tablespoons dark rum

Grated fresh coconut
12 fresh figs, stemmed and sliced

Soften the gelatin in ¼ cup of the milk. Set aside.

Scald the remaining 1½ cups milk in the top of a double boiler. Stir in the sugar, salt, and the gelatin mixture. Cook over hot water, stirring, until the gelatin and sugar have dissolved. Set aside.

Beat the egg yolks. Beat in 2 tablespoons of the hot milk mixture, and then add the egg yolks to the mixture in the top of the double boiler. Cook, stirring constantly, until the mixture thickens slightly. Remove from the heat, cool, then stir in the rum. Refrigerate until almost set.

❖❖

Beat the egg whites until stiff, and fold into the cooled custard. Spoon into 6 individual dessert molds and keep in the refrigerator until firm. Sprinkle 6 dessert plates with fresh coconut, unmold the rum creams onto the middle of the plates, and arrange slices of the fresh figs around the cream. Top with a little more coconut and serve.

Yield: 6 servings

Brandied Peaches in Cream

❖❖❖

When you are buying peaches, first look for a rosy color. Then smell them to see if they are really ripe. The ripe ones smell like a peach and make you want to eat them. The peaches that aren't ripe usually smell like the packaging they came in.

6 large ripe peaches
¼ cup peach brandy
2 tablespoons powdered sugar
1 envelope unflavored gelatin
2 tablespoons cold water
½ cup white sugar
2 cups whipping cream
1 teaspoon vanilla extract
2 tablespoons cognac

Peel and slice 4 of the peaches. Put them in a mixing bowl, pour the brandy over them, sprinkle the powdered sugar on top, and mix gently. Chill in the refrigerator for 1 hour.

Mix the gelatin in the cold water. Combine with the white sugar and 1 cup of the whipping cream in a saucepan and cook over low heat, stirring constantly, until the gelatin and sugar dissolve. Cool well.

Whip the remaining 1 cup whipping cream until stiff. Fold into the gelatin mixture along with the vanilla.

Drain the peaches, reserving the liquid, and arrange in a 1½-quart mold. Pour the gelatin mixture over them and chill in the refrigerator for at least 4 hours.

◆◆

While the gelatin mixture chills, peel the remaining 2 peaches and chop. Combine in a blender with the cognac and the reserved sugar/peach brandy liquid. Blend well.

To serve, unmold the gelatin onto a serving plate and pour the peach sauce over top. Serve at once.

Yield: 6 to 8 servings

Oranges & Cream

❖❖

1 cup sugar
1 tablespoon all-purpose flour
1 egg
1 cup water
1 cup whipping cream
4 oranges, peeled, sectioned, and chopped

Combine the sugar, flour, egg, and water in a double boiler. Cook over hot water, stirring constantly, until thick. Cool.

Beat the whipped cream until stiff. Fold into the cooled custard. Place the orange pieces in 4 dessert cups or bowls, pour the cream mixture over them, and serve.

Yield: 4 servings

Crème avec Fraises Cointreau

Why is it everything tastes better and seems more elegant with a French name attached? In one of my restaurants when we served Chicken à la King, it didn't sell; but when it was Chicken à la Reine, it sold out. Cream with Strawberries and Cointreau will be a best-seller no matter what you call it.

4 cups milk
8 egg yolks
1 cup granulated sugar
¾ cup all-purpose flour
½ teaspoon vanilla extract
1 quart strawberries
2 tablespoons powdered sugar
¼ cup Cointreau or other orange-
   flavored liqueur
Garnish: Whipped cream, fresh mint,
   and orange twists

Scald the milk. Beat the egg yolks and the white sugar until pale yellow. Beat in the flour, and then gradually beat in the hot milk. Cook in a saucepan over medium heat, beating constantly with a whisk until smooth and thick. Remove from the heat and stir in the vanilla. Chill.

Wash, hull, and slice the strawberries; place in a bowl. Stir the powdered sugar into the Cointreau, pour over the strawberries, and toss lightly. Chill for 1 hour.

Just before serving, spoon the cream into 6 individual dessert dishes, then spoon the strawberries over the cream. Top each dish with whipped cream; garnish with a sprig of fresh mint and a twist of orange.

Yield: 6 servings

45

Strawberries with Sauterne Custard

Rich, golden Sauterne gives this custard a wonderful fruity flavor. I recommend using an American Sauterne, which usually is a lot drier than a French Sauternes (the French retain the "s" even in the singular). If you use a French wine, you might want to slightly reduce the amount of sugar you add to accommodate the extra sweetness of the wine.

2 tablespoons sugar
1 pint medium-sized strawberries,
  washed and hulled
2 tablespoons kirsch
4 egg yolks
½ cup sugar
½ cup Sauterne wine

Sprinkle the 2 tablespoons sugar over the strawberries, stir in the kirsch, and let stand at room temperature for an hour.

In the top of a double boiler, beat the egg yolks with the ½ cup sugar until thick. Cook over boiling water, beating constantly and slowly adding the wine, until the mixture is a light yellow and has tripled in volume, about 10 minutes. Remove from the heat and place the top of the double boiler in a bowl filled with ice water. Beat the mixture until well chilled.

Pour into 4 individual dessert dishes, top with the strawberries, and serve.

Yield: 4 servings

Bourbon Custard with Fruit

❖❖❖

1 medium-sized ripe cantaloupe
1 pint blueberries
4 egg yolks
½ cup sugar
⅛ teaspoon salt
¼ teaspoon ground nutmeg
1¾ cups milk
¼ cup bourbon
1 cup heavy cream
1 tablespoon sugar
Blueberry preserves (select an "all-fruit" brand)

Peel, seed, and cut the cantaloupe into bite-sized cubes. Wash and pick over the blueberries. Mix the fruit together and arrange in 6 individual dessert cups.

Beat the egg yolks with the ½ cup sugar in a heavy-bottomed saucepan. Add the salt and the nutmeg. Add the milk. Cook over medium heat, stirring constantly, until the mixture begins to thicken. Remove from the heat and add the bourbon. Cool; then pour over the fruit.

Beat the cream until peaks start to form. Add the remaining 1 tablespoon sugar and continue to beat until stiff peaks form. Spoon on top of the Bourbon Custard, dot with the blueberry preserves, and serve.

Yield: 6 servings

Raspberries with Kahlua Custard

◆◆◆

6 egg yolks
½ cup sugar
1½ cups milk
½ cup Kahlua
2 tablespoons extra strong brewed
  coffee
1 pint raspberries
¼ cup raspberry liqueur
2 tablespoons sugar
1 cup whipping cream
Garnish: Mint leaves

Beat the egg yolks, then add the ½ cup sugar and continue beating with a wire whisk until smooth. Pour the milk into a saucepan, add the Kahlua and coffee, and heat just to the boiling point. Do not let boil! Slowly add the hot milk mixture to the egg yolks and sugar, beating constantly.

Return the mixture to the saucepan and cook over low heat, stirring constantly, until the mixture coats the back of a spoon. Cool.

While the custard cools, combine the raspberries, liqueur, and remaining 2 tablespoons sugar. Chill in the refrigerator for at least 1 hour.

Just before serving, whip the cream until stiff and fold into the cooled custard. Spoon

◆◆◆

into 6 to 8 individual shallow dessert dishes. Gently strain the liquid from the berries and spoon the berries on top of the custard. Garnish with mint leaves and serve.

Yield: 6 to 8 servings

Spiced Pears with Winter Custard

◆◆

The custard is deceptively simple. The cool, fresh taste of the lime plays well off the spiced pears and the bite of Mirabelle, a French plum liqueur.

Winter Custard

1 envelope unflavored gelatin
¼ cup cold water
½ cup sugar
1 cup hot water
⅔ cup lime juice
1 teaspoon lime zest
4 egg whites
¼ cup sugar
Plum Sauce (page 117)
Garnish: Fresh mint or thinly sliced
    lemon twists

Spiced Pears

4 ripe pears
1 teaspoon ground nutmeg
½ teaspoon ground mace
¼ teaspoon ground cinnamon
¼ teaspoon ground cardamom
1 cup pear nectar
1 tablespoon lemon juice

To make the custard, mix the gelatin with the cold water in a large mixing bowl. Stir in the ½ cup sugar and the hot water until the gelatin is completely dissolved. Stir in the lime juice and zest. Chill in the refrigerator, stirring occasionally, until the mixture has the consistency of unbeaten egg whites.

Beat the egg whites until they start to

form peaks. Beat in the remaining ¼ cup sugar, and continue to beat until stiff peaks form. Fold in the gelatin and mix well. Spoon the custard into a lightly greased mold and refrigerate until set (overnight is best).

To make the spiced pears, peel, core, and slice the pears. Mix the spices with the pear nectar and lemon juice and pour over the pears. Chill for at least 3 hours.

To serve, unmold the custard onto a platter and arrange the spiced pears on top and around the sides. Pour the Plum Sauce over the custard and pears and garnish with sprigs of mint or twists of lemon.

Yield: 6 servings

Fresh Pineapple with Almond Cream

The marriage of almond-flavored liqueur with pineapple doesn't need a prenuptial contract because it's such a natural. I have found that using a boning knife makes the job of peeling a pineapple very easy.

Almond Cream

2 envelopes unflavored gelatin
1¾ cups water
2 cups milk
¾ cup sugar
¼ cup Amaretto or other almond-flavored liqueur
1 medium-sized pineapple
Garnish: Sliced almonds

Pineapple Almond Sauce

1 cup canned crushed pineapple in unsweetened juice, with the juice
2 tablespoons finely chopped slivered, blanched almonds
2 tablespoons Amaretto or other almond-flavored liqueur

To make the almond cream, soften the gelatin in ¼ cup of the water. Combine the remaining 1½ cups water with the milk and sugar in a saucepan. Cook over low heat, stirring occasionally, until the sugar has dissolved. Stir the gelatin and the liqueur into the mixture. Pour into a 9-inch-square dish and chill in the refrigerator until the mixture is set.

◆◆

To make the sauce, combine the canned crushed pineapple and juice, the chopped almonds, and the liqueur in a blender and blend until smooth.

Peel the pineapple and slice into 1-inch-thick vertical slices. Cut the slices into triangles to make pineapple spears.

Cut the gelatin into 6 squares, then cut the squares into triangles. Place 2 triangles, point to point, in each of 6 shallow dessert dishes, and arrange the pineapple spears around the edges. Pour the Pineapple Almond Sauce over top. Garnish with sliced almonds and serve.

Yield: 6 servings

Papaya with Vanilla Cream

◆◆

1 cup whipping cream
3 egg yolks
3 tablespoons sugar
1 tablespoon cornstarch
1 teaspoon vanilla extract
1 cup fresh apricots, peeled and pitted
1 cup sugar
2 tablespoons apricot brandy
½ cup shredded, dried, unsweetened
  coconut
1 tablespoon light rum
4 large papayas

In the top of a double boiler over hot (but not boiling) water, heat the cream.

In a separate bowl, beat the egg yolks. Stir in the 3 tablespoons sugar and cornstarch. Add the vanilla and then gradually stir the egg mixture into the cream. Beat constantly with a wire whisk until the custard thickens. Remove from the heat and place the top of the double boiler in a bowl of ice water. Beat with a whisk until cool. Refrigerate for at least 3 hours.

Prepare an apricot glaze by combining the apricots and the remaining 1 cup sugar in a saucepan. Mash the apricots into the sugar and bring to a boil over medium high heat (watch the mixture closely so that it doesn't boil over). Simmer the mixture for

♦♦

15 to 20 minutes. Run the mixture through a strainer and stir in the apricot brandy. Refrigerate for at least 3 hours.

About 30 minutes before serving, combine the coconut and rum and set aside.

To serve, cut the papayas in half and remove the seeds. Peel and cut into slices. Spoon the Vanilla Cream onto 6 to 8 flat dessert dishes or plates and arrange the papaya slices in a circle around the cream. Top with the apricot glaze and sprinkle with the rum-flavored coconut.

Yield: 6 to 8 servings

Airy Pudding with Grand Marnier

I discovered this pudding in a very old cookbook. Although I'm not sure, I feel that it might be English in origin. I adapted the recipe to modern cooking methods, but I kept the name because I think it aptly describes this light, chiffon-like dessert. This makes the perfect end to a heavy meal when you want just a taste of something sweet and light.

¾ cup sugar
1 envelope unflavored gelatin
1¼ cups boiling water
¼ cup lemon juice
1 egg white
1 teaspoon grated lemon zest
Grand Marnier Sauce (page 126)

Combine the sugar and gelatin in a mixing bowl. Stir in the boiling water and lemon juice and mix until the gelatin is dissolved. Chill in the refrigerator for 30 minutes, or until the mixture starts to gel. Add the egg white and beat until the mixture has doubled in volume. Fold the lemon zest into the pudding.

Spoon into 8 individual serving dishes and chill until firm. Serve with the Grand Marnier Sauce poured over the pudding.

Yield: 8 servings

4
Mousses

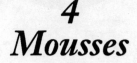

Café Provençal's Chocolate Mousse

When beating egg whites for any mousse, you will find they peak best if the whites are brought up to room temperature first I prefer to use a metal bowl, either stainless steel or copper. Do not try to beat egg whites with one drop of the egg yolk in them. They will not beat well or form good peaks.

1 pound semisweet chocolate
3 tablespoons unsalted butter
6 eggs, separated
¼ cup brandy
1 teaspoon vanilla extract
½ teaspoon cream of tartar
2 cups heavy cream, very cold
Garnish: Brandy-flavored whipped
  cream and shaved chocolate

Melt together the chocolate and butter in the top of a double boiler over medium heat. When they have melted, cool.

Beat the egg yolks until a light lemon yellow color. Beat the brandy and vanilla into the egg yolks. Then beat the mixture very, very slowly into the cooled chocolate. Set aside.

Beat the egg whites until they start to form peaks. Add the cream of tartar and continue beating until they form stiff peaks. Set aside.

Beat the cream until it forms stiff peaks. Fold the egg whites and the cream alternately into the chocolate. Spoon into 6 to 8 individual stemmed dessert dishes or wine glasses and chill in the refrigerator for at

❖❖

least 2 hours.

To serve, top each mousse with a dollop of whipped cream laced with the same type of brandy used in the recipe and sprinkle on some shaved chocolate.

Although this particular recipe calls for semisweet chocolate, you can use half un-sweetened and half semisweet, which makes a very lovely mousse.

Yield: 6 to 8 servings

White Chocolate Almond Mousse

❖❖❖

1 envelope unflavored gelatin
¼ cup cold water
2 cups whipping cream
12 ounces white chocolate
2 tablespoons Amaretto or other
   almond-flavored liqueur
4 eggs
½ cup chopped almonds
Raspberry Wine Sauce (page 115)
2 cups canned mandarin oranges

Sprinkle the gelatin over the water in a saucepan. Place over low heat and stir until the gelatin is dissolved. Stir in 1 cup of the cream and bring just to the boiling point. Do not boil! Pour the mixture into a blender. Add the chocolate and blend until the chocolate has melted. Slowly add the remaining 1 cup of the cream and the liqueur. Blend in the eggs. Stir in the almonds. Chill for 1 hour.

About 1 hour before serving, spread 8 to 10 dessert plates with the raspberry sauce. Spoon the mousse into the center of the plates and chill for another hour.

To serve, arrange the oranges around the edges and center of the mousse.

Yield: 8 to 10 servings

Maple Mousse

◆◆◆

My father came from a long line of inventors and was an extremely inventive person himself. Without one maple tree on our property, he decided to produce maple syrup and soon became one of the largest producers in our area. Needless to say we had lots of the sweet stuff around the house, and my mother was always coming up with ways to use it. This is one of my favorites.

6 eggs, separated
1 cup pure maple syrup
½ teaspoon cream of tartar
1 pint heavy cream

Beat the egg yolks and combine with the maple syrup in a saucepan. Cook over low heat, stirring occasionally, until the mixture just comes to a boil. Do not let it boil. Remove from heat. Let cool for 30 minutes.

Beat the egg whites until almost stiff, add the cream of tartar, and continue beating until the egg whites are stiff.

Beat the cream until it forms peaks. Fold the cream and then the egg whites into the maple syrup mixture. Spoon into an ungreased 1½-quart mold and chill for at least 4 hours.

To serve, unmold the mousse by immersing the bottom of the mold in hot water for a minute or two. Then invert onto a serving dish.

Yield: 4 to 5 servings

Café au Lait Mousse

❖❖❖

4 egg whites
1 pint heavy cream
½ cup sugar
1 tablespoon unflavored gelatin
5 tablespoons strong brewed coffee

Beat the egg whites until very stiff. Beat the cream until it just begins to form peaks. Slowly beat the sugar into the whipped cream and then fold into the egg whites. Dissolve the gelatin in the coffee and then gradually fold into the cream and egg white mixture. Spoon into 4 individual stemmed dessert dishes or wine glasses and chill for at least 2 hours before serving.

Yield: 4 servings

Crème de Menthe Mousse

❖❖❖

I was just completing this book as St. Patrick's Day approached. Knowing that this time of year brings out the Irish in me, my wife brought me a pot of shamrocks for my desk and made the following mousse for dinner because it is green. It was so good I decided to include it in the book.

2 envelopes unflavored gelatin
2½ cups milk
3 eggs, separated
¾ cup sugar
Pinch salt
¼ cup green crème de menthe
1 cup whipping cream
Garnish: orange zest

Stir the gelatin into ½ cup of the milk and set aside. Heat 1 cup of the milk to the boiling point and add to the gelatin mixture. Stir to dissolve the gelatin. Add the remaining 1 cup of cold milk, the egg yolks, sugar, salt, and crème de menthe and beat well.

Beat the egg whites until stiff.

In a separate bowl, beat the whipping cream until stiff. Fold the egg whites and the whipping cream, alternately, into the crème de menthe mixture. Spoon into 6 to 8 individual dessert dishes or wine glasses. Sprinkle a little orange zest on top and chill for at least 3 hours before serving.

Yield: 6 to 8 servings

Eggnog Mousse

❖❖❖

It is traditional during the Christmas season in New Mexico to outline one's rooftops and/or walkways with sand-filled paper sacks in which a votive candle is placed. The candles are lit every night during the yuletide season. Once inside the home, visitors are served all sorts of Christmas cheer, including this one.

1 tablespoon unflavored gelatin
¼ cup dark rum
¾ cup water
¼ cup brandy
1 egg
4 ice cubes
5 tablespoons sugar
1 teaspoon vanilla extract
1½ cups ricotta cheese
¼ teaspoon ground nutmeg
¼ teaspoon ground cinnamon

Mix the gelatin and rum in a blender. Heat the water and brandy until it just comes to a boil. Pour into the blender and blend until the gelatin is dissolved. Add the egg and the ice cubes and blend until the ice is melted. Add the sugar, vanilla, ricotta cheese, nutmeg, and cinnamon; blend until the mixture is smooth.

Pour into a lightly greased 2-quart mold and chill for at least 4 hours, or until set. Unmold onto a plate and garnish with holly or red and green maraschino cherries.

Yield: 6 servings

Apricot Mousse

❖❖

**2½ pounds ripe apricots, pitted and
  peeled**
1 cup sugar
2 tablespoons brandy
¼ cup sweet white wine
1 cup heavy cream
4 egg whites
2 tablespoons sugar

Puree the apricots in a blender. Mix the apricots with the 1 cup sugar, the brandy, and wine. Set aside.

Whip the cream until it forms stiff peaks. Beat the egg whites until they form stiff peaks, adding the remaining 2 tablespoons sugar as you beat them. Alternately fold the egg whites and whipped cream into the apricot mixture.

Spoon into 8 to 10 individual dessert dishes. Garnish with additional whipped cream, if desired.

Yield: 8 to 10 servings

Mango Mousse

◆◆

4 egg yolks
1 cup heavy cream
½ cup sugar
1 envelope unflavored gelatin
2 tablespoons water
6 large ripe mangoes or 1 (# 303) can
   mangoes, with the juice
1 cup sweet white wine (if using the
   canned mangoes use just enough
   wine with the mango juice to make
   1 cup liquid)
1 cup whipping cream
6 tablespoons Apricot Sauce (page 116)

In a saucepan, beat the egg yolks. Then beat in the heavy cream and sugar. Cook over low heat until warm.

Soften the gelatin in the water. Stir the gelatin into the egg and cream mixture and continue to cook until the gelatin dissolves and the mixture starts to thicken. Do not let it boil! Remove from the heat and cool.

Peel, pit, and slice the mangoes. Combine with the wine in a blender and process until the mangoes are pureed. Fold the mango mixture into the cooled custard and refrigerate until the mixture starts to thicken.

Whip the whipping cream until it forms stiff peaks and fold into the mango mixture. Spoon into a 1½-quart mold that has been

◆◆◆

sprayed with a natural vegetable oil coating; cover and chill in the refrigerator for 4 hours, or until set.

Unmold onto a serving plate and drizzle with the Apricot Sauce before serving.

Yield: 6 servings

Peach Mousse

❖❖

4 egg yolks
½ cup milk
½ cup heavy cream
½ cup sugar
2 envelopes unflavored gelatin
2 tablespoons water
6 large ripe peaches
1 cup sweet white wine
1 cup heavy cream
Raspberry Sauce (page 114)

In a saucepan, beat the egg yolks. Then beat in the milk, the ½ cup heavy cream, and sugar. Cook over low heat until warm.

Soften the gelatin in the water, then stir into the egg and cream mixture, and continue to cook until the gelatin dissolves and the mixture starts to thicken. Do not let it boil! Remove from the heat and cool.

Peel, pit, and slice the peaches. Combine in a blender with the wine and blend until the peaches are pureed. Fold the peaches into the cooled custard and refrigerate until the custard starts to thicken.

Whip the remaining 1 cup heavy cream until it forms stiff peaks, and fold into the peach custard.

Spoon into a 2-quart mold that has been

◆◆

sprayed with a natural vegetable oil coating; cover and chill in the refrigerator for 4 hours, or until set.

Unmold onto a serving plate and drizzle with the Raspberry Sauce before serving.

Yield: 6 servings

Rhubarb Mousse

◆◆◆

I am very fond of rhubarb, but I get tired of the same old rhubarb and strawberry pie, or stewed rhubarb. This is a refreshing change.

Mousse
1 pound rhubarb, cut into 1-inch pieces
½ cup cold water
½ cup sugar
1 envelope unflavored gelatin
¼ cup strawberry liqueur (or ¼ cup
   strawberry preserves mixed with 2
   teaspoons brandy)
4 egg whites
1 pint heavy cream
¾ cup sugar

Strawberry Glaze
4 tablespoons strawberry jam
2 tablespoons brandy

To make the mousse, in a saucepan, combine the rhubarb with the water and the ½ cup sugar. Cook over low heat for 45 minutes, or until the rhubarb becomes very soft.

Soften the gelatin in the liqueur or the brandy and then stir into the hot rhubarb. Let cool.

Beat the egg whites until stiff. Beat the cream, adding the remaining ¾ cup sugar a little at a time, until the cream forms stiff peaks. Fold the whipped cream and the egg whites alternately into the rhubarb mixture.

Spoon into a 2-quart mold that has been

sprayed with a natural vegetable oil coating. Chill in the refrigerator for at least 3 hours.

To make the glaze, mix together the jam and the brandy in a saucepan and cook over very low heat until smooth. Cool.

To serve, unmold the mousse onto a serving platter and drizzle the Strawberry Glaze over the top.

Yield: 4 to 6 servings

Holiday Cranberry Mousse

This goes over big at a holiday party!

1 pound fresh or frozen cranberries
¼ cup water
1 cup sugar
1 tablespoon unflavored gelatin
¼ cup cranberry juice
4 egg whites
1 pint heavy cream
½ cup sugar

Cook the cranberries, water, and the 1 cup sugar over low heat until the cranberries are soft. Cool, puree in a blender, then strain.

Dissolve the gelatin in the cranberry juice and stir into the cranberry puree.

Beat the egg whites until they form stiff peaks. Beat the cream until it just starts to form peaks. Add the remaining ½ cup sugar to the cream, and beat until it forms stiff peaks. Fold the cream and egg whites alternately into the cranberry mixture.

Spoon into a festive serving dish or mold and chill in the refrigerator for at least 4 hours. Garnish with Christmas greenery and serve.

Yield: 4 to 6 servings

Easy Frozen Lemon Mousse

Nothing could be simpler! Remember when using fresh lemon or lime juice, if you put the fruit in the microwave on high for just a couple of seconds, it will yield a lot more juice.

2 cups heavy cream
½ cup sugar
½ cup lemon juice
½ teaspoon grated lemon zest
Chocolate Sauce (page 121)
Garnish: Thinly sliced lemon twists

Beat the cream until it forms stiff peaks. Fold the sugar into the cream, then fold in the lemon juice and lemon zest. Spoon into a 9-inch by 5-inch loaf pan that has been sprayed with a natural vegetable oil coating and freeze until firm.

To serve, put a little Chocolate Sauce in the center of 8 dessert plates, and place a slice of lemon mousse on top of it. Garnish with a twist of thinly sliced lemon.

Yield: 8 servings

Frozen Cantaloupe Mousse

❖❖

½ cup crème de cassis
3 tablespoons sugar
2 cups peeled and cubed cantaloupe
2 cups whipping cream
Dash salt
Raspberry Wine Sauce (page 115)

Mix together the crème de cassis and sugar and pour over the cantaloupe. Let stand at room temperature for 1 hour. Pour into a blender and puree.

Whip the cream with the salt until it forms soft peaks, and fold into the cantaloupe mixture. Pour into a 2-quart mold that has been sprayed with a natural vegetable oil coating and freeze until firm. Unmold and serve with the Raspberry Sauce on the side.

Yield: 4 to 6 servings

Frozen Pumpkin Mousse

This recipe is for people who are avoiding cream in their diets. Yogurt replaces the cream.

1½ cups cooked mashed or pureed pumpkin
½ cup milk
1 teaspoon pumpkin pie spice mix
¼ teaspoon ground nutmeg
1 cup sugar
1 quart plain yogurt

Mix together the pumpkin, milk, spices, and sugar. Fold in the yogurt. Spoon into 8 individual dessert dishes that will withstand freezer cold. Freeze until firm. This is delicious served with gingersnaps and chocolate curls.

Yield: 8 servings

Frozen Brandy Mousse

❖❖

8 eggs, separated
¾ cup sugar
½ cup brandy
2 cups heavy cream
Raspberry Wine Sauce (page 115)
Chocolate Sauce (page 121)

Combine the egg yolks and sugar in the top of a double boiler and cook over boiling water for 10 minutes, beating or whisking all the time. Remove from the heat. Stir the brandy into the mixture and cool for 10 minutes.

Beat the egg whites until stiff. Beat the cream until stiff. Fold the cream and egg whites alternately into the custard. Spoon into an ungreased 1½-quart mold and freeze until firm.

To serve, unmold onto a plate that has been coated with Raspberry Wine Sauce. Drizzle Chocolate Sauce over the top of the mousse.

Yield: 8 servings

5
Baked Custards, Flans, & Puddings

Old-Fashioned Cup Custard

This is what food writers are now describing as comfort food. The secret to making most custards is to make sure they set up without burning. Putting the custard cups or molds into a pan of shallow hot water is usually the answer. I put in just enough water to come halfway up the custard cup and then check it midway in the baking process.

2 cups milk
¼ cup sugar
⅛ teaspoon salt
4 egg yolks
½ teaspoon vanilla extract
Garnish: Nutmeg

Preheat the oven to 325° F.

Scald the milk in a saucepan, then add the sugar and salt and mix well. Beat the egg yolks and pour the scalded milk mixture over them very, very slowly. Stir in the vanilla. Pour the custard into 6 individual custard cups. Place the cups in a shallow pan partially filled with hot water and bake for 25 minutes, or until the custard is set. Sprinkle a little nutmeg on top while the custard is still warm. Serve warm or cold.

Yield: 6 servings

Scandinavian Custard

◆◆◆

When I was a child we had a family ritual of going to my father's hometown to visit his sisters for the Christmas holidays. My aunt followed the Swedish tradition of preparing a large smorgasbord on Christmas Eve. This custard was one of the desserts that was served every year.

2 cups milk
1 cup firmly packed light brown sugar
⅛ teaspoon salt
4 egg yolks
½ teaspoon vanilla extract
⅛ teaspoon ground anise
Garnish: Finely chopped candied fruit

Preheat the oven to 325° F.

Scald the milk and then stir in the brown sugar and salt. Beat the egg yolks very well and pour the scalded milk mixture into them very slowly, beating constantly. Add the vanilla and anise and mix well. Pour into 6 individual custard cups. Place the cups in a shallow pan partially filled with hot water and bake for 25 to 30 minutes, or until the custard is set. While the custard is still warm, sprinkle a little finely chopped candied fruit over the top and serve.

Yield: 6 servings

79

Chocolate Custard

❖❖

I have a friend who told me he didn't like custard. "Custard ranks right up there with chicken soup and ginger ale in my book," he told me, "things you only eat when you're sick." I served him this chocolate custard, and he decided that custard was for the healthy after all.

4 cups milk
4 eggs
⅓ cup sugar
2 tablespoons unsweetened cocoa
   powder
¼ teaspoon salt
1 teaspoon vanilla extract
Garnish: Shaved white chocolate

Preheat the oven to 325° F.

Scald the milk. Beat the eggs very well, and then stir in the sugar, cocoa, and salt. While stirring the egg mixture, slowly pour the scalded milk into it. Stir in the vanilla. Pour into 8 individual custard cups. Place the cups in a shallow pan partially filled with hot water and bake for 45 minutes, or until the custard is set. Serve chilled, garnished with shaved white chocolate curls.

Yield: 8 servings

Coconut Custard

❖❖

Here is an old-fashioned, made-from-scratch recipe. The orange zest really gives this dessert that little something extra.

½ cup dried white bread crumbs
½ cup grated, dried, sweetened coconut
2 cups milk
3 tablespoons sugar
½ tablespoon butter, melted
1 egg, beaten
½ teaspoon grated orange zest

Preheat the oven to 325° F. Lightly grease an 8-inch-square baking pan.

Put the bread crumbs in a mixing bowl. Stir in the coconut. Pour the milk over top and let the mixture soak until the bread becomes soft. Mix in the sugar and melted butter. Add the egg and mix well. Pour the custard into the baking dish. Sprinkle the orange zest on top. Set the baking dish in a larger pan partially filled with hot water and bake for 30 minutes, or until set. Serve cooled.

Yield: 4 to 6 servings

Ginger Pudding

My grandmother, Japhet, had a passion for ginger. She used it a lot, and this pudding was one of her favorite desserts. She also had a succession of orange-colored cats, and all of them were called Ginger.

3 eggs
½ teaspoon salt
2 tablespoons sugar
2 tablespoons melted butter
⅔ cup fresh bread crumbs
1½ teaspoons finely chopped ginger
   root
½ cup milk
1 teaspoon vanilla extract
Rum Sauce (page 125)
Garnish: Chopped walnuts

Preheat the oven to 350° F.

Beat the eggs very well. Mix in the salt, sugar, butter, bread crumbs, ginger, milk, and vanilla. Spoon into 4 individual molds or custard cups. Set in a shallow pan partially filled with hot water and bake for 30 minutes, or until set. Cool for about 10 minutes.

Unmold onto individual dessert plates that have been lightly covered with Rum Sauce. Sprinkle lightly with chopped walnuts and serve.

Yield: 4 servings

Pumpkin Custard

❖❖❖

2 cups cooked, mashed, or pureed
  pumpkin pulp
4 eggs
¾ cup milk
¼ cup all-purpose flour
¾ cup honey
¼ teaspoon salt
2 teaspoons vanilla extract
¼ teaspoon ground cloves
¼ teaspoon ground nutmeg
¼ teaspoon ground cinnamon
¼ teaspoon ground mace
¼ teaspoon ground allspice
Garnish: Bourbon-flavored whipped
  cream

Preheat the oven to 400° F.

Combine the pumpkin, eggs, milk, flour, honey, salt, vanilla, and spices in a blender and blend well. Pour into a 2-quart baking dish. Then place the dish in a larger pan partially filled with hot water. Bake for 1 hour, or until set. Chill. Serve topped with whipped cream laced with bourbon.

Yield: 8 servings

Lemon Chiffon Pudding

❖❖

A light and wonderful pudding, this is perfect for a summertime dessert. The trick to this dish is to use freshly squeezed lemon juice.

3½ tablespoons flour
⅔ cup sugar
2 tablespoons butter, at room temperature
3 eggs, separated
3 tablespoons lemon juice
⅔ cup milk

Preheat the oven to 350° F.

Mix together the flour and sugar. Blend the butter with the flour and sugar mixture. Beat the egg yolks and stir into the mixture. Add the lemon juice and milk, and mix well.

Beat the egg whites until stiff, and fold into the mixture. Spoon into 6 individual custard cups and bake for 35 minutes, or until set. Chill well before serving.

Yield: 6 servings

Applesauce Meringue Pudding

I like to make my own applesauce for this dish. Before you throw up your hands in dismay and run to the store for a jar of your favorite brand, let me tell you how easy it is. Just peel, core, and quarter some tart apples, cover with water in a saucepan, bring to a boil, and cook just until tender. Add sugar to taste, stir well, and store in the refrigerator.

3 eggs, separated
3 cups applesauce
¼ teaspoon vanilla extract
¼ teaspoon almond extract
⅛ teaspoon salt
6 tablespoons sugar
½ teaspoon vanilla extract

Preheat the oven to 300° F.

Beat the egg yolks. Then add the applesauce. Mix the ¼ teaspoon vanilla extract, almond extract, and salt into the applesauce mixture. Pour into an 8-inch-square baking dish.

Beat the egg whites until they start to stiffen, then gradually add the sugar and the remaining ½ teaspoon vanilla. Continue to beat until the egg whites form stiff peaks. Spoon the meringue on top of the pudding, making sure to touch all sides of the dish. Place the baking dish in a larger pan and pour hot water into the larger pan until it reaches halfway up the sides of the 8-inch baking dish. Bake for about 20 minutes, or until lightly browned. Serve warm.

Yield: 4 servings

Orange Meringue Pudding

❖❖

Cream of tartar added to egg whites will help make them stiffer and retain their peaks. Make sure the egg whites touch the sides of the baking dish, mold, or pie crust all the way around to prevent shrinkage.

6 medium-sized oranges
2 tablespoons white sugar
6 eggs, separated
1 cup white sugar
4 cups milk
2 teaspoons cornstarch
¼ cup orange-flavored liqueur
¼ teaspoon cream of tartar
¾ cup powdered sugar
2 tablespoons water
1 teaspoon vanilla extract

Preheat the oven to 325° F.

Peel and section the oranges, removing all the white membranes and seeds. Place the sections in the bottom of a 2-quart baking dish. Sprinkle the 2 tablespoons white sugar over the oranges.

In the top of a double boiler, beat the egg yolks until lemon colored. Beat the remaining 1 cup white sugar and milk into the egg yolks. Stir the cornstarch into the liqueur, mix well, and then stir into the egg mixture. Place the double boiler over hot water and cook until thickened. Pour over the orange sections.

Beat the egg whites until they start to stiffen. Add the cream of tartar. Add the powdered sugar, a little at a time, and

◆◆

continue to beat the egg whites until they form stiff peaks. Mix together the water and vanilla, and beat into the egg whites. Spoon the meringue over the orange pudding, making sure to touch all sides of the dish. Bake for about 20 minutes, or until the meringue is lightly browned. Serve warm.

Yield: 6 servings

Mexican Flan

◆◆

Often called the national dessert of Mexico, this is also the way we make it in New Mexico.

1 cup firmly packed light brown sugar
2 egg whites
2 teaspoons vanilla extract
¾ cup white sugar
4 egg yolks
2 (12-ounce) cans evaporated milk

Preheat the oven to 350° F.

Divide the brown sugar equally among 4 custard cups. Put the cups in a large pan that has enough water to come halfway up the side of the cups. Bring the water to a boil on top of the stove. When the sugar has melted and turned a golden brown color, take a pair of kitchen tongs and tilt the cups until the caramelized sugar coats the inside of the cup about halfway up. Remove the cups from the water and let them cool.

Beat the egg whites until they form peaks, then beat in the vanilla and white sugar. Beat the egg yolks and beat them into the mixture. Then gradually beat in the milk.

Pour the flan into the sugar-coated custard cups. Place the cups in a shallow

❖❖

baking pan partially filled with about an inch of water. Bake for 1 hour. Turn the custards out onto 4 small serving plates and cool before serving.

Yield: 4 servings

Gringo Flan

❖❖❖

This is the way Norte Americanos make flan.

4 eggs
¼ cup sugar
¼ teaspoon salt
1 teaspoon vanilla extract
3 cups milk
6 tablespoons pure maple syrup

Preheat the oven to 350° F.

Beat the eggs, and then stir in the sugar, salt, and vanilla. Scald the milk and slowly stir it into the mixture. Pour 1 tablespoon maple syrup into the bottom of each of 6 custard cups and spoon the custard mixture over the top of the syrup. Place the custard cups in a shallow pan partially filled with hot water. Bake for 1½ hours, or until set. Cool before serving.

Yield: 6 servings

Devil's Food Pudding

When you dip your spoon into this I'm sure you are going to agree that it is aptly named—it is ever so sinful tasting!

⅓ cup butter
⅓ cup unsweetened cocoa powder
½ cup boiling water
1 cup sugar
2 eggs
¼ cup milk
1 cup all-purpose flour
½ teaspoon salt
1 teaspoon baking powder
1 teaspoon vanilla extract
½ cup chopped walnuts
Garnish: Whipped cream flavored with
   crème de menthe, peppermint
   schnapps, or mint extract

Preheat the oven to 400° F. Spray a 1½-quart baking dish with a natural vegetable oil coating.

Mix together the butter and cocoa and stir in the boiling water. Then add the sugar and stir until smooth. Set aside.

Beat the eggs and add to the milk. Set aside.

Sift together the flour, salt, and baking powder. Mix into the cocoa mixture, alternating with the milk and egg mixture. Add the vanilla and nuts; mix well.

Pour the pudding into the baking dish, cover, and bake for about 45 minutes, or until set. Serve cooled with mint-flavored whipped cream.

Yield: 6 to 8 servings

91

Fudge Upside-Down Pudding

I came across this in an old family recipe file.

1 cup all-purpose flour
2 teaspoons baking powder
½ teaspoon salt
¾ cup white sugar
2 tablespoons unsweetened cocoa
   powder
½ cup milk
1 teaspoon vanilla extract
2 tablespoons melted butter
1 cup firmly packed light brown sugar
1 cup chopped pecans
4 tablespoons unsweetened cocoa
   powder
1¾ cups hot water

Preheat the oven to 350° F. Lightly butter a 2-quart baking dish.

Sift together the flour, baking powder, salt, white sugar, and the 2 tablespoons cocoa. Stir in the milk, vanilla, and butter. Pour into the baking dish. Mix together the brown sugar, pecans, and remaining 4 tablespoons cocoa. Sprinkle on top of the batter. Pour the hot water over the entire batter.

Bake for 45 minutes, or until a knife inserted into the center comes out clean. Cool for 15 minutes, then invert onto a serving plate. This is delicious served with whipped cream.

Yield: 6 servings

Persimmon Pudding

◆◆

The persimmon is a soft, golden-orange fruit. It will take about 2 dozen persimmons to produce 2 cups of pulp, which you can obtain by peeling the fruit and pressing the flesh through a sieve.

2 cups persimmon pulp
1 cup sugar
½ cup sour milk or buttermilk
½ teaspoon baking soda
1 cup all-purpose flour
¼ cup melted butter
2 eggs, lightly beaten
½ cup sugar
¼ cup water
½ cup orange-flavored liqueur
1 cup chopped pecans
Garnish: Whipped cream

Preheat the oven to 350° F. Lightly butter an 8-inch-square baking dish.

Mix together the persimmon, the 1 cup sugar, the sour milk, baking soda, flour, and melted butter. Stir in the eggs lightly. Pour the pudding into the baking dish and bake for 30 minutes.

While the pudding bakes, mix together the remaining ½ cup sugar, water, and liqueur. Remove the pudding from the oven and poke holes in the top. Pour the sauce over the pudding so that it runs into the holes. Return to the oven and bake for another 30 minutes. Cut into squares and serve warm or cold with whipped cream.

Yield: 4 to 6 servings

Cherry Pudding

❖❖

1 cup all-purpose flour
½ teaspoon ground cinnamon
1¼ cups sugar
1 teaspoon baking soda
¼ teaspoon salt
2 tablespoons butter, melted
2 eggs, beaten
3 cups pitted sour cherries
½ cup chopped pecans
Cherry Cider Sauce (page 119)

Preheat the oven to 350° F. Lightly grease an 8-inch-square baking dish.

In a large bowl, mix together the flour, cinnamon, sugar, baking soda, and salt. Stir in the butter and eggs. Stir in the cherries and mix well.

Pour into the baking dish, sprinkle the pecans on top, and bake for 45 minutes. Serve with the cherry sauce.

Yield: 6 servings

6
Bread & Rice Puddings

Bread Pudding with Pecans

❖❖

We live in pecan country. Until I moved out West, I used mostly walnuts in my cooking. But with pecan trees in the backyard, I soon started substituting pecans—and found that they work just as well, if not better, in most recipes.

**4 cups bread crumbs (stale bread is
    best for this recipe)**
1 cup sugar
3 cups milk
1 cup seedless raisins
1 cup chopped pecans
1 tablespoon lemon juice
3 tablespoons vanilla extract
1 teaspoon ground cinnamon
1 teaspoon ground mace
Kentucky Hard Sauce (page 129)

Preheat the oven to 350° F. Lightly grease a 2-quart baking dish.

Combine all of the ingredients, except the hard sauce, and pour into the baking dish. Bake for 1 hour, or until the pudding is firm. Serve warm or cold with the hard sauce passed on the side.

Yield: 8 servings

Rich Bread Pudding

❖❖

A grizzled old cook told me, "Gimme butter, cream, sugar, and a little whiskey and I can make ya' anything." Then he gave me this recipe. "There isn't any whiskey in this," I said. "Kid, that other stuff's fer the pot— the whiskey's for me!"

4 eggs
1 cup white sugar
2 tablespoons light brown sugar
1 teaspoon ground nutmeg
¼ cup butter, melted
3 cups heavy cream
4 cups stale white bread, torn small
1 cup seedless golden raisins
Vanilla Cream Sauce (page 124)

Beat the eggs lightly. Stir both sugars and the nutmeg into the eggs and beat. Add the butter. Stir in the cream and mix well. Stir the bread and raisins into the mixture and let stand for 30 minutes.

Preheat the oven to 375° F. Lightly butter a 2-quart baking dish.

Pour the pudding into the baking dish and bake for 1 hour, or until the top is brown. Serve warm with the Vanilla Cream Sauce passed on the side.

Yield: 8 servings

Orange Bread Pudding

Orange marmalade gives this bread pudding its delightful flavor. Use the best marmalade you can find, preferably an Irish brand. This makes a terrific addition to Sunday breakfast and goes well with afternoon tea on a rainy day.

6 slices stale white bread
3 tablespoons butter, at room
   temperature
1 cup orange marmalade
4 eggs
2 cups milk
2 teaspoons lemon juice
1 teaspoon ground nutmeg
Whiskey Sauce (page 120)

Preheat the oven to 300° F. Lightly butter an 8-inch-square baking dish.

Lightly toast the bread, then butter it. Spread the marmalade on the buttered toast. Cut the toast into 1-inch cubes, then put the cubes in the baking dish.

Lightly beat the eggs; then beat in the milk, lemon juice, and nutmeg. Pour over the bread cubes and bake for 45 minutes, or until firm. Serve hot or cold, pouring some sauce over each serving.

Yield: 4 to 6 servings

Chocolate Bread Pudding

I have found that even people who turn up their noses at plain bread pudding as being too pedestrian can't resist this one made with chocolate.

2 cups evaporated milk
2 cups water
2 tablespoons butter
2 cups bread crumbs made with slightly stale bread
3 eggs
1 cup sugar
¼ cup unsweetened cocoa powder
1 teaspoon vanilla extract
¼ teaspoon salt

Preheat the oven to 350° F. Lightly butter an 8-inch-square baking dish.

Combine the milk and water in a saucepan. Add the butter and heat over high heat until the milk begins to scald. Put the bread crumbs into a bowl and pour the hot liquid over them. Set aside.

Lightly beat the eggs; then beat in the sugar, cocoa, vanilla, and salt. Combine with the bread mixture. Pour into the baking dish and bake for 45 minutes, or until firm. Serve hot or cold.

Yield: 6 servings

Blueberry Bread Pudding

◆◆◆

4 cups fresh blueberries
¼ cup all-purpose flour
4 cups milk
6 slices white bread, torn into cubes
¼ teaspoon salt
1 teaspoon cinnamon
1 cup sugar
¾ cup shredded, dried, sweetened
  coconut
2 tablespoons butter

Wash and drain the berries. Put the berries in a mixing bowl and lightly toss with the flour. Let stand for 30 minutes.

Preheat the oven to 350° F. Lightly butter a 2-quart baking dish.

Scald the milk. Pour over the bread cubes. Stir in the salt, cinnamon, sugar, and coconut. Add the berries and pour into the baking dish. Dot the top with the butter and bake for 45 minutes. Serve warm with French vanilla ice cream or Vanilla Cream Sauce (page 124).

Yield: 6 to 8 servings

Lemon Rice Pudding

1 cup cooked white rice
2 tablespoons butter
1 tablespoon lemon zest
¼ cup lemon juice
2 cups milk
2 egg yolks
¼ cup sugar
3 egg whites
1 tablespoon lemon juice
½ cup sugar

Preheat the oven to 350° F.

Mix together the rice, butter, lemon zest, and the ¼ cup lemon juice. Heat the milk and stir into the mixture. Beat the egg yolks and add. Stir in the ¼ cup sugar. Spoon into an 8-inch-square baking dish; set the baking dish in a larger pan partially filled with hot water. Bake for 30 minutes.

Beat the egg whites until they form stiff peaks. Fold in the remaining 1 tablespoon lemon juice and ½ cup sugar. Remove the pudding from the oven and spread the meringue over the top, being sure to seal the edges to the dish. Return to the oven just long enough to brown the meringue, 10 to 15 minutes. Serve cooled.

Yield: 4 to 6 servings

Peach Rice Pudding

6 eggs, beaten
1½ cups cooked white rice
¼ teaspoon salt
½ cup sugar
2 teaspoons vanilla extract
1½ teaspoons grated lemon zest
3½ cups milk
2 cups sliced fresh peaches
1 tablespoon freshly squeezed lemon
    juice
2 tablespoons brandy
1 cup shredded, dried, sweetened
    coconut

Preheat the oven to 350° F. Lightly butter a 2-quart baking dish.

Combine the eggs with the rice, salt, sugar, vanilla, lemon zest, and milk. Pour into the baking dish. Set the dish in a larger pan partially filled with hot water. Bake for 1 hour, or until the pudding is set. Cool.

Meanwhile, combine the peaches, lemon juice, brandy, and coconut; chill.

To serve, spoon the chilled peaches on top of the cooled pudding.

Yield: 8 to 10 servings

Palm Springs Rice Pudding

Many years ago, I was a weekend guest at a friends' home in Palm Springs where they served this pudding after dinner. They were kind enough to give me the recipe. If you can find Seville oranges, use them; they give this dish a nice twist.

3 oranges
1½ cups miniature marshmallows
1 tablespoon sugar
1 cup chopped dates
2 cups cooked long-grain white rice
1 cup heavy cream
Garnish: Orange slices

Peel the oranges, remove the seeds, and chop the fruit into small pieces, saving the juice. Mix the marshmallows with the orange pieces and juice. Stir in the sugar. Add the dates and the rice.

Beat the cream until it is thick and fold it into the pudding. Spoon into 8 individual dessert dishes and chill. Garnish with orange slices and serve.

Yield: 8 servings

Orange Rice Pudding Glacé

❖❖

3 cups cooked white rice
3 cups milk
½ cup sugar
¼ teaspoon salt
1 tablespoon orange marmalade
1 teaspoon vanilla extract
1 teaspoon ground nutmeg
1 cup sour cream
2 tablespoons sugar
1 tablespoon orange liqueur
1 teaspoon grated orange zest

In a saucepan, mix together the rice, milk, the ½ cup sugar, and the salt. Cook over medium-high heat, stirring often, until the mixture is thick and creamy. This will take about 30 minutes. Remove from the heat and stir in the marmalade, vanilla, and nutmeg. Pour into a 2-quart baking dish. Mix together the sour cream, the remaining 2 tablespoons sugar, liqueur, and orange zest. Spread this over the rice mixture, put under the broiler just long enough to glaze, and serve.

Yield: 6 to 8 servings

7
Steamed Puddings

Steamed Blueberry Pudding

❖❖❖

2 cups all-purpose flour
4 teaspoons baking powder
½ teaspoon salt
2 tablespoons sugar
2 tablespoons butter
1 cup milk
2 tablespoons molasses
1 cup blueberries
Enough all-purpose flour to coat the
   blueberries

Sift together the 2 cups flour and baking powder; mix in the salt and sugar. Cut in the butter, and then mix in the milk and molasses. Coat the blueberries lightly with flour and add them to the mixture.

Pour the pudding into a lightly greased 1-quart ring mold. Cover with aluminum foil and poke 8 to 10 small holes in the foil. Set on a wire rack in a pan of hot water, with enough water to come up the sides of the mold about 2 inches. Steam for 1½ hours, or until firm. Add more water if necessary.

To serve, unmold the pudding onto a serving plate. Place a bowl of powdered sugar in the center of the mold and sprinkle a little over each serving.

Yield: 6 servings

Steamed Fig Pudding

¾ cup dried figs
¾ cup butter, at room temperature
1 cup sugar
3 eggs, beaten
2 cups all-purpose flour
1 teaspoon baking soda
1 teaspoon ground mace
1 teaspoon ground cinnamon
½ teaspoon salt
½ cup milk
1 teaspoon vanilla extract
Lemon Sauce (page 118), warmed

Run the figs through a grinder or food processor and coarsely grind. In a medium-sized bowl, cream together the butter and sugar. Add the figs. Stir in the eggs.

Sift together the flour, baking soda, mace, cinnamon, and salt. Stir in the milk and mix well. Add the egg and fig mixture and the vanilla. Pour into 6 to 8 custard cups. Cover with aluminum foil and poke a few small holes in the foil. Set the cups on a wire rack in a pan of hot water, with enough water to come up the sides of the cups about 1 inch. Steam for 45 minutes, or until firm. Add more water to the pan if necessary. Serve warm with warmed Lemon Sauce poured over each serving.

Yield: 6 to 8 servings

Steamed Applesauce Pudding

2½ cups all-purpose flour
1 teaspoon salt
½ teaspoon baking soda
1½ teaspoons baking powder
1 teaspoon ground cinnamon
½ teaspoon ground ginger
½ cup finely ground suet
¾ cup seedless raisins
½ cup chopped nuts
1 cup fine dried bread crumbs
½ cup light molasses
2 eggs, well beaten
1 cup applesauce
Orange Hard Sauce (page 127)

In a large bowl, sift together the flour, salt, baking soda, baking powder, cinnamon, and ginger. Add the ground suet, raisins, nuts, and bread crumbs. Combine the molasses, eggs, and applesauce. Fold into the flour mixture and stir well.

Grease and sugar a 1½-quart mold by lightly rubbing the inside of the mold with butter or spraying with a natural vegetable oil coating. Tip the mold up and lightly sprinkle granulated sugar on the sides, rotating the mold until the entire inside surface is coated with sugar. Then lightly sprinkle the sugar on the bottom of the mold. Pour the pudding into the mold. Cover the mold with aluminum foil. Using a sharp knife, poke 8 to 10 small holes in the foil. Set the mold on a wire rack in a pan of hot water, with enough water to come up the sides of the mold about 2 inches. Steam for 2½ hours, or until firm. Check the water in the pan a few times as the pudding steams, and add more water if necessary. Serve warm with Orange Hard Sauce passed on the side.

Yield: 8 to 10 servings

Christmas Plum Pudding

Plum pudding is an English Christmas tradition said to have been created by Daga, the ancient Celtic god of plenty, to celebrate the winter solstice. From the fourteenth century on, this pudding has been an important part of yuletime feasting. Prior to raisins becoming popular in England, prunes were used in the pudding, but neither prunes nor plums are ever used in today's versions.

1 cup seedless raisins
1 cup dried currants
½ pound suet
1½ cups all-purpose flour
½ teaspoon baking soda
1 teaspoon ground cinnamon
½ teaspoon ground nutmeg
¼ teaspoon ground ginger
¼ teaspoon ground allspice
½ cup bread crumbs, made from stale bread
1 cup firmly packed light brown sugar
1 teaspoon lemon zest
1 teaspoon orange zest
½ cup chopped candied lemon peel
½ cup chopped candied orange peel
1 cup chopped walnuts
4 eggs, lightly beaten
¾ cup milk
1 teaspoon vanilla extract
2 tablespoons dark rum
Spiced Hard Sauce (page 128) or
    Orange Hard Sauce (page 127)

Combine the raisins and currants with hot water to cover. Set aside to plump for 30 minutes. Finely grind the suet in a meat grinder or food processor. Set aside. Grease a 2-quart mold.

Sift the flour, baking soda, cinnamon, nutmeg, ginger, and allspice into a large bowl. Add the bread crumbs, brown sugar, the zest and candied citrus peels, walnuts, and suet to the bowl. Drain the raisins and currants and add to the mixture. Stir in the eggs. Add the milk, vanilla, and rum. Stir the ingredients together very well. Spoon the mixture into the mold. Cover tightly with pierced aluminum foil and place the mold on a wire rack in a large pan of hot water, with enough water to come halfway up the side of the mold. Cover the pan and steam for 5 hours over low heat.

Serve hot with a hard sauce passed on the side. The pudding can be stored in the refrigerator for up to 5 weeks. To serve after refrigeration, wrap the pudding in a cloth and steam to warm through, or warm it in a microwave oven.

Yield: 12 servings

Steamed Cranberry Pudding

❖❖❖

The combination of the corn syrup and molasses gives this dish a unique richness as well as a truly old-fashioned flavor. It doesn't sound all that sweet, until you put the cream sauce on it. The combination is just right.

¼ cup dark molasses
¼ cup light corn syrup
2 teaspoons baking soda
⅓ cup hot water
1⅓ cups all-purpose flour
2 cups fresh or frozen whole
   cranberries
Rich Cream Sauce (page 123)

Mix together the molasses, corn syrup, baking soda, hot water, flour, and cranberries in the top of a double boiler and stir. Place over hot water and cook for 1 hour.

Spray a 1-quart mold with oil and pour the pudding into the mold. Cover with aluminum foil. Using a sharp knife, poke 8 to 10 small holes in the foil. Set the mold on a wire rack in a pan of hot water, with enough water to come up the sides of the mold about 2 inches. Steam for 1¼ hours, or until firm. Add more water if necessary.

To serve, unmold onto a serving platter and pass the cream sauce on the side. Serve warm.

Yield: 4 to 6 servings

8
Dessert Sauces

Raspberry Sauce

•••

This versatile sauce is excellent, not only on Peach Mousse, but also with Chocolate Bread Pudding, Lemon Chiffon Pudding, and Café au Lait Mousse. In addition, you can use it to top off your favorite ice cream.

1 cup raspberry juice
2 teaspoons cornstarch
1 cup currant jelly

Mix a little of the raspberry juice with the cornstarch to make a paste. Combine with the rest of the raspberry juice and the currant jelly in a saucepan and bring to a rolling boil. Cook until the sauce thickens and is clear. Cool in the refrigerator before serving.

Yield: Approximately 2 cups

Raspberry Wine Sauce

❖❖

Spoon this marvelous sauce onto a dessert plate and then place a serving of Chocolate Bavarian Cream on top of it. Or serve with Chocolate Custard, Frozen Lemon Mousse, or Cantaloupe Mousse. I particularly like it spooned over some Lime Curd and then topped with fresh raspberries to intensify the taste of raspberry. I often make this sauce, substituting a semisweet white wine for the red wine. Then I spread the sauce between the layers of a rich chocolate cake before icing it.

1 cup ripe raspberries
¾ cup sugar
¾ cup red wine
1 teaspoon grated orange zest

Combine all the ingredients in a saucepan and bring to a boil, stirring occasionally and mashing the berries. When the sugar has melted, cool and strain. Chill in the refrigerator for at least 3 hours before serving.

Yield: Approximately 2 cups

Apricot Sauce

The Tuaca liqueur that flavors this sauce has been made for over 5 centuries in Italy. First created during the Renaissance, this golden amber liqueur has a hint of vanilla and orange in it. In addition to using Tuaca in this sauce, put a little elegance in your bedtime hot chocolate by adding some Tuaca. This liqueur is available in most good liquor stores. Try this sauce on Mango Mousse, Chocolate Bavarian Cream, Apricot Mousse, Chocolate Custard, and Rich Bread Pudding.

½ cup apricot preserves
½ cup Tuaca liqueur
Pinch salt

Mix all of the ingredients in a saucepan and cook over very low heat until smooth. Cool before serving.

Yield: Approximately ¾ cup

Plum Sauce

❖❖

Use sweet red or purple plums for this sauce, which couples the sweet richness of the plum with the bite of the Mirabelle. Although not easy to find, Mirabelle liqueur is available in specialty wine and liquor stores. If you or any of your friends are going to Europe, put this on your wish list. It is extraordinary! The sauce complements many of the desserts in this book, including the Café au Lait Mousse, Chocolate Custard, Rich Bread Pudding, Minted Grapes, and the Frozen Cantaloupe Mousse.

6 medium-sized red or purple fresh or canned plums, peeled and pitted
2 teaspoons Mirabelle (French plum liqueur)

Combine the plums and the liqueur in a blender and blend until smooth. Serve at room temperature.

Yield: Approximately ½ cup

Lemon Sauce

◆◆◆

This is a wonderful all-purpose sauce. I use it with all sorts of desserts, including raspberry sherbet. Try it spooned over Kahlua Cream, Mango Mousse, Rich Bread Pudding, Steamed Fig Pudding, or the Christmas Plum Pudding—to name just a few of the desserts it complements.

½ cup sugar
3 tablespoons all-purpose flour
3 egg yolks
¾ cup cold water
¾ cup lemon juice
1 tablespoon unsalted butter
Zest of ½ lemon

In the top of a double boiler, combine the sugar and flour. Beat the egg yolks with the water and then stir into the sugar mixture. Cook over hot water for 10 minutes, stirring constantly. Add the lemon juice, butter, and lemon zest; stir and heat through. This is good served either hot or cold.

Yield: Approximately 2 cups

Cherry Cider Sauce

❖❖❖

I originally came up with this recipe to go with the Cherry Pudding in this book. Then I discovered that it was superb served cold over Steamed Fig Pudding, Steamed Applesauce Pudding, Devil's Food Pudding, and Rich Bread Pudding. Try it as one of the sauces for a banana split. It wonderfully offsets hot fudge.

1 tablespoon cornstarch
½ cup sugar
¼ teaspoon salt
1 cup cherry cider or cherry wine
2 tablespoons butter
½ teaspoon almond liqueur

Combine the cornstarch, sugar, and salt and dissolve in the cherry cider. Cook in a saucepan over low heat, stirring constantly, until clear. Add the butter and the almond liqueur and continue cooking over very low heat until the sauce thickens. Serve cold.

Yield: Approximately 1 cup

Whiskey Sauce

The uses are too numerous to list for this sauce, which derives its unique flavor from good bourbon. Taste it on Ginger Pudding or with Peach Mousse. It's good with chocolate anything, including double fudge chocolate ice cream. I also like it on Christmas Plum Pudding as an alternative to a hard sauce.

½ cup butter
1 cup sugar
1 egg
½ cup bourbon or blended whiskey

Cream the butter and sugar together and cook over medium high heat in the top of a double boiler until the sugar dissolves. Remove from the heat and cool. Beat the egg and add to the cooled mixture. Stir the whiskey into the mixture and serve.

Yield: Approximately 1½ cups

Chocolate Sauce

This is good chocolate sauce. The tequila makes it a little unusual.

½ cup butter
½ cup milk
1 cup powdered sugar
¼ cup unsweetened cocoa powder
1 tablespoon golden tequila
1 teaspoon vanilla extract

Melt the butter in the milk in a saucepan over very low heat (or in a microwave oven). Remove from the heat, add the sugar and cocoa, and beat until smooth. Add the tequila and vanilla; beat again. Serve at room temperature.

Yield: Approximately 1 cup

Chocolate Caramel Sauce

Serve this rich sauce hot with Pears René or any poached pear. Pour over French vanilla ice cream and sprinkle a few chopped walnuts on top for a delightful treat. It also makes an interesting combination with Easy Frozen Lemon Mousse and seems to be a natural over Bread Pudding with Pecans. It might seem like gilding the lily, but spooned over Chocolate Bread Pudding, it is sheer delight.

2 ounces unsweetened chocolate
2 cups firmly packed light brown sugar
2 tablespoons butter
½ cup heavy cream
½ teaspoon vanilla extract

Melt the chocolate in the top of a double boiler over hot water, or in a microwave oven. Stir in the brown sugar and mix well. Add the butter, cream, and vanilla. Cook until the mixture is blended and smooth. Serve hot.

Yield: Approximately 1 cup

Rich Cream Sauce

◆◆

This sauce provides an added richness to most steamed puddings, including Steamed Fig Pudding, Steamed Applesauce Pudding, and Steamed Cranberry Pudding. I can't imagine a bread pudding it wouldn't go with, but I like it best with Chocolate Bread Pudding.

½ cup butter, at room temperature
1 cup sugar
¾ cup heavy cream
1 teaspoon vanilla extract
8-ounce package cream cheese, at room temperature

Combine all of the ingredients in a saucepan and bring to a boil. Reduce the heat and cook, stirring constantly, until the sauce is smooth. Serve at room temperature.

Yield: Approximately 1 cup

Vanilla Cream Sauce

The perfect marriage with many bread puddings, including Chocolate Bread Pudding and Bread Pudding with Pecans, this sauce is also excellent over a wide array of steamed puddings, especially those with fruit, such as figs, apples, and cranberries.

2 eggs
1½ cups heavy cream
3 tablespoons light brown sugar
½ cup white sugar
1 tablespoon all-purpose flour
2 teaspoons vanilla extract
½ teaspoon ground nutmeg
2 tablespoons unsalted butter, melted

Lightly beat the eggs, and then mix together with the remaining ingredients. Cook over medium heat, stirring occasionally, until the sauce has thickened. Serve warm.

Yield: Approximately 2 cups

Rum Sauce

❖❖

One of the most versatile of sauces, this pairs well with steamed puddings, custards, fruit mousses, and cream desserts. It is a natural with Ginger Pudding. Try spooning it onto a dessert plate and then placing Frozen Rum Cream in the center of it, and garnishing with some candied fruit.

2 eggs, lightly beaten
1 cup heavy cream
½ cup sugar
1 tablespoon all-purpose flour
1 teaspoon vanilla extract
2 tablespoons unsalted butter, melted
2 tablespoons light rum

Combine the eggs with the cream, sugar, flour, and vanilla in a saucepan. Stir in the melted butter. Cook over medium heat, stirring occasionally, until the sauce has thickened. Stir in the rum. Cool to room temperature before serving.

Yield: Approximately 2 cups

Grand Marnier Sauce

What wouldn't this be good on? It complements such diverse desserts as Christmas Plum Pudding, Airy Pudding, and White Chocolate Almond Mousse. Try drizzling a little on assorted melon balls, or use it in place of whipped cream to top off strawberry shortcake.

3 egg yolks
½ cup sugar
Pinch salt
½ cup milk
½ cup heavy cream
½ cup Grand Marnier

Beat together the egg yolks, sugar, and salt in a mixing bowl. Combine the milk and cream in a saucepan and bring just to a boil. Gradually beat the hot milk mixture into the egg yolks, using a wire whisk. Return to the saucepan and cook over low heat, stirring occasionally, until the mixture coats a spoon. Beat the Grand Marnier into the sauce and chill before serving.

Yield: Approximately 2 cups

Orange Hard Sauce

❖❖❖

I find that topping my steamed puddings or bread puddings with hard sauce shaped with a small ice cream scoop or a large melon baller makes a very attractive dish. Try spreading some Raspberry Sauce on a dessert plate, a hot wedge of Bread Pudding with Pecans on it, and top it off with this sauce.

½ cup butter
1½ cups powdered sugar
2 tablespoons orange-flavored liqueur
2 teaspoons orange zest

Mix all of the ingredients together and chill in the refrigerator for at least 2 hours before serving.

Yield: Approximately 2 cups

Spiced Hard Sauce

❖❖

The addition of the spices to this hard sauce makes it the perfect accompaniment to bread puddings and steamed puddings.

¼ cup butter, at room temperature
2 cups powdered sugar
¼ teaspoon ground allspice
¼ teaspoon ground nutmeg
¼ teaspoon ground cinnamon

Cream together the butter and the sugar. Stir in the spices and chill for at least 1 hour before serving.

Yield: Approximately 2 cups

Kentucky Hard Sauce

❖❖❖

Plum Pudding crowned with this hard sauce can make any meal memorable. Or, substitute this sauce for the whipped cream suggested in the Bananas with Butterscotch recipe. I also can't think of many more pleasant tastes than this hard sauce on top of warm gingerbread.

¼ cup butter, at room temperature
1 cup powdered sugar
¼ cup Kentucky sippin' whiskey
   (bourbon)

Mix all of the ingredients together and chill in the refrigerator for at least 2 hours before serving.

Yield: Approximately ½ cup

Wine Sauce

✦✦

Serve this cold wine sauce on Rich Bread Pudding or with Almond Custard. It is delicious on cold, sliced fruit such as apples, pears, and melon. Drizzle a little over lemon pound cake for a quick and easy dessert.

2 tablespoons butter
2 tablespoons sugar
1 cup dry red wine

Melt the butter in a small saucepan. Stir in the sugar. Then stir in the wine and cook for 10 minutes over very low heat. Remove from the heat. Serve chilled.

Yield: Approximately 1 cup

Index

◆◆◆

A

Airy Pudding with Grand Marnier, 56
Almond Cream, Fresh Pineapple with, 52–53
Almond Custard, 33
Applesauce Meringue Pudding, 85
Applesauce Pudding, Steamed, 108–109
Apricot Mousse, 65
Apricot Sauce, 116

B

Baked custards
    Chocolate, 80
    Coconut, 81
    Ginger Pudding, 82
    Gringo Flan, 90
    Mexican Flan, 88–89
    Old-Fashioned, 78
    Pumpkin, 83
    Scandinavian, 79

Bananas
    with Butterscotch, 15
    Jamaican, 13
    Jungle Cry, 14
Bavarian Cream, Chocolate, 30–31
Benedictine Strawberries, 10
Black Cherries with Zabaglione, 39
Blackberries à la Viscount, 12
Blueberries
    Bread Pudding, 100
    and Cantaloupe with Bourbon
        Custard, 47
    Steamed Pudding, 106
Bourbon Custard, 23
    Blueberries and Cantaloupe with, 47
Brandied Peaches in Cream, 42–43
Brandy Mousse, Frozen, 76
Bread Pudding, 4
    Blueberry, 100

Chocolate, 99
Orange, 98
with Pecans, 96
Rich, 97
Butterscotch, Bananas with, 15

C

Café au Lait Mousse, 62
Café Provençal's Chocolate Mousse, 58–59
Cantaloupe
    and Blueberries with Bourbon
        Custard, 47
    Mousse, Frozen, 74
    and Raspberries, Lime Curd with, 11
Caramel Sauce, Chocolate, 122
Caribbean Chocolate Custard, 29
Cherries
    Black, with Zabaglione, 39
    Cider Sauce, 119
    Pudding, 94
Chocolate
    Bavarian Cream, 30–31

Bread Pudding, 99
Caramel Sauce, 122
Custard, 28, 29, 80
Devil's Food Pudding, 91
Fudge Upside-Down Pudding, 92
Mousse, Cafe Provencal's, 58–59
Pots de Crème, 22
Sauce, 121
White, Almond Mousse, 60
Christmas Plum Pudding, 110–111
Coconut Custard, 81
Cranberry Mousse, Holiday, 72
Cranberry Pudding, Steamed, 112
Creams, 3
    Almond, Fresh Pineapple with, 52–53
    Brandied Peaches, 42–43
    Chocolate Bavarian, 30–31
    Crème Brûlée, 24
    Crème avec Fraises Cointreau, 45
    Frozen Rum, 25
    Kahlua, 32
    Madeira, 26–27

Oranges and, 44
Rum, Fresh Figs with, 40–41
with Strawberries and Cointreau, 45
Vanilla, Papaya with, 54–55
Cream Sauce, 123–124
Crème de Menthe Mousse, 63
Crèmes, 3. See also Creams
Custards, 3
Almond, 33
Bourbon, 23
Blueberries and Cantaloupe with, 47
Chocolate, 28, 29
Bavarian, 30–31
Crème Brûlée, 24
Floating Island, 34–35, 36
Frozen Rum Cream, 25
Kahlua, Raspberries with, 48–49
Madeira Cream, 26–27
Pots de Crème, 22
Sabayon, 20
Sauterne, Strawberries with, 46
Winter, Spiced Pears with, 50–51

Zabaglione, 21
See also Baked custards; Creams; Crèmes; Sabayon; Zabaglione

D
Devil's Food Pudding, 91

E
Easy Frozen Lemon Mousse, 73
Eggnog Mousse, 64

Fig Pudding, Steamed, 107
Figs, Fresh, with Rum Cream, 40–41
Flan, 88–89, 90
Floating Island, 34–35, 36
Frozen Mousse
Brandy, 76
Cantaloupe, 74
Lemon, 73
Pumpkin, 75
Frozen Rum Cream, 25

Fruit, 2–3
    Bananas with Butterscotch, 15
    Benedictine Strawberries, 10
    Blackberries à la Viscount, 12
    Blueberries and Cantaloupe with Bourbon Custard, 47
    Brandied Peaches in Cream, 42–43
    Crème avec Fraises Cointreau, 45
    Fresh Figs with Rum Cream, 40–41
    Fresh Pineapple with Almond Cream, 52–53
    Jamaican Bananas, 13
    Jungle Cry, 14
    Lime Curd with Cantaloupe and Raspberries, 11
    Melon with Rum Sabayon, 38
    Minted Grapes, 17
    Oranges and Cream, 44
    Papaya with Vanilla Cream, 54–55
    Pears René, 18
    Raspberries with Kahlua Custard, 48–49
    Spiced Pears with Winter Custard, 50–51

    Strawberries
        and Kiwi with Lemon Curd, 8
        Romanoff, 9
        with Sauterne Custard, 46
    Triple Orange Threat, 16
Fudge Upside-Down Pudding, 92

G

Ginger Pudding, 82
Grand Marnier Sauce, 126
Grapes, Minted, 17
Gringo Flan, 90

H

Hard Sauce, 127–129
Holiday Cranberry Mousse, 72

J

Jamaican Bananas, 13
Jungle Cry, 14

K

Kahlua Cream, 32
Kahlua Custard, Raspberries with, 48–49
Kentucky Hard Sauce, 129
Kiwi with Lemon Curd, Strawberries and, 8

L

Lemon
    Chiffon Pudding, 84
    Curd, Strawberries and Kiwi with, 8
    Mousse, Easy Frozen, 73
    Rice Pudding, 101
    Sauce, 118
Lime Curd with Cantaloupe and
    Raspberries, 11

M

Madeira Cream, 26–27
Mango Mousse, 66–67
Maple Mousse, 61
Melon. See also Cantaloupe
    with Rum Sabayon, 38

Mexican Flan, 88–89
Minted Grapes, 17
Mousse, 4
    Apricot, 65
    Brandy, Frozen, 76
    Cafe Provencal's Chocolate, 58–59
    Café au Lait, 62
    Cantaloupe, Frozen, 74
    Cranberry, Holiday, 72
    Crème de Menthe, 63
    Eggnog, 64
    Lemon, Easy Frozen, 73
    Mango, 66–67
    Maple, 61
    Peach, 68–69
    Pumpkin, Frozen, 75
    Rhubarb, 70–71
    White Chocolate Almond, 60

O

Old-Fashioned Cup Custard, 78
Oranges
    Bread Pudding, 98
    and Cream, 44
    Hard Sauce, 127
    Meringue Pudding, 86–87
    Rice Pudding Glacé, 104
    Triple Orange Threat, 16

P

Palm Springs Rice Pudding, 103
Papaya with Vanilla Cream, 54–55
Peaches
    Brandied, in Cream, 42–43
    Mousse, 68–69
    Rice Pudding, 102
Pears René, 18
Pears, Spiced, with Winter Custard, 50–51
Pecans, Bread Pudding with, 96
Persimmon Pudding, 93

Pineapple, Fresh, with Almond Cream, 52–53
Plum Pudding, Christmas, 110–111
Plum Sauce, 117
Pots de Crème, 22
Puddings, 4–5
    Airy with Grand Marnier, 56
    Applesauce Meringue, 85
    Cherry, 94
    Devil's Food, 91
    Fudge Upside-Down, 92
    Ginger, 82
    Lemon Chiffon, 84
    Orange Meringue Pudding, 86–87
    Persimmon, 93
    See also Custards; Rice Pudding;
    Steamed Pudding
Pumpkin Custard, 83
Pumpkin Mousse, Frozen, 75

R

Raspberries
    with Kahlua Custard, 48–49
    Lime Curd with Cantaloupe and, 11
    Sauce, 114, 115
Rhubarb Mousse, 70–71
Rice Pudding, 4
    Lemon, 101
    Orange, 104
    Palm Springs, 103
    Peach, 102
Rich Bread Pudding, 97
Rich Chocolate Custard, 28
Rich Cream Sauce, 123
Rum
    Cream, Fresh Figs with, 40–41
    Cream, Frozen, 25
    Sabayon, Melon with, 38
    Sauce, 125

S

Sabayon, 3–4, 20
    Rum, Melon with, 38
Sauces, 5–6
    Apricot, 116
    Cherry Cider, 119
    Chocolate, 121, 122
    Grand Marnier, 126
    Hard, 127–129
    Lemon, 118
    Plum, 117
    Raspberry, 114, 115
    Rich Cream, 123
    Rum, 125
    Vanilla Cream, 124
    Whiskey, 120
    Wine, 115, 130
Sauterne Custard, Strawberries with, 46
Scandinavian Custard, 79
Spiced Hard Sauce, 128
Spiced Pears with Winter Custard, 50–51
Steamed puddings, 4

Applesauce, 108–109
Blueberry, 106
Christmas Plum, 110–111
Cranberry, 112
Fig, 107
Strawberries
Benedictine, 10
Crème avec Fraises Cointreau, 45
and Kiwi with Lemon Curd, 8
Rhubarb Mousse, 70–71
Romanoff, 9
with Sauterne Custard, 46

T

Triple Orange Threat, 16

V

Vanilla Cream, Papaya with, 54–55
Vanilla Cream Sauce, 124

W

Whiskey sauces, 120, 129
White Chocolate Almond Mousse, 60
Wine Sauce, 115, 130
Winter Custard, Spiced Pears with, 50–51

Z

Zabaglione, 3, 21
Black Cherries with, 39

OTHER SPECIALTY COOKBOOKS FROM THE CROSSING PRESS

SAUCES FOR PASTA! By Kristie Trabant	$8.95	**SUN-DRIED TOMATOES!** By Andrea Chesman	$8.95
PESTOS! By Dorothy Rankin	$8.95	**SALSAS!** By Andrea Chesman	$8.95
PASTA SALADS! By Susan Janine Meyer	$8.95	**GOOD FOR YOU COOKIES!** By Jane Marsh Dieckmann	$8.95
SALAD DRESSINGS! By Jane Marsh Dieckmann	$8.95	**OLD WORLD BREADS!** By Charel Steele	$8.95
FRUIT DESSERTS! By Dorothy Parker	$8.95	**SORBETS!** By Jim Tarantino	$8.95

FAST BREADS!
By Howard Early and
   Glenda Morris
	$8.95	**BROWNIES, BARS,
		   AND BISCOTTI!**
		   By Terri Henry
			$8.95

CONDIMENTS! By Jay Solomon	$8.95	**LOW CHOLESTEROL DESSERTS!** By Terri J. Siegel	$8.95

Available at your local bookstore, or write directly to The Crossing Press, P. O. Box 1048, Freedom, CA 95019. Please add $2.00 for postage on the first book, and $.50 for each additional book. If you wish, you may use VISA or MASTERCARD. Please give your number and expiration date.

We publish many more cookbooks. Please write or call TOLL FREE 800/777-1048 for a free catalog.